Before she gets her period

Talking with
your daughter
about menstruation

Jessica B. Gillooly, PhD

Illustrations by Nery Orellana

Perspective Publishing
Los Angeles

Library of Congress Catalogue Card Number 98-12087
ISBN: 0-9622036-9-6

Published by Perspective Publishing, Inc.
2528 Sleepy Hollow Dr. #A, Glendale, CA 91206
800-330-5851; perspectivepub@loop.com
www.familyhelp.com

Additional copies of this book may be ordered by calling toll free
1-800-330-5851, or by sending $17.95 (13.95 + $4 shipping) to
above address. CA residents add 8.25% ($1.15) sales tax. Discounts
available for quantity orders. Bookstores, please call LPC Group at
1-800-626-4330.

Gillooly, Jessica B., 1947–
    Before she gets her period: talking with your daughter about
    menstruation / Jessica B. Gillooly ; illustrations by Nery Orellana.
        p. cm.
    Includes bibliographical references and index.
    ISBN 0-9622036-9-6 (pbk.)
    1. Menarche. 2. Menstruation. 3. Girls—Health and hygiene.
4. Girls—Growth. 5. Girls—Physiology. 6. Sex instruction for
girls. 7. Mothers and daughters. I. Title.
RJ145.G54   1998
612.6'62—dc21

Illustrations by Nery Orellana
Back cover photo by Linda Goodman Pillsbury
Printed in the United States of America
Second printing: 1999

Acknowledgments

With immense gratitude and appreciation I thank my daughter, Heather, and my husband, Greg, for their initial commitment, continued support, repeated sacrifices and their final practical words, "We'll take care of everything around the house, just get it done!" Without Heather's loving ways, enormous patience, and exuberance for life, I would never have begun. Without Greg's loving words of encouragement, his belief that I could write this book, and help every step of the way, I would not have finished this book. I will be forever thankful to both of you for allowing me the privilege to write and struggle through my first manuscript. I am truly blessed.

To Linda Pillsbury, who devoted untold hours of reading the many drafts, who saw a book among all the pages, whose patience was phenomenal and who didn't give up on me when others (probably every other publisher) would have, sincerely I thank you. You are gifted at giving direction, encouragement, and friendship.

I thank my dear friend Wanda Johnson, who started this project with me many years ago in our Psychology of Women classes. This was well before we thought about a book as the way to share the wonderful stories we were reading. Your insights, laughter, final gift of your work to this project and commitment to our twenty years of friendship means more than I can express. And to Briana, her daughter, a special thanks for sharing your mother, your story, and your developing years.

To all the individuals who wrote their intimate stories and trustingly shared them, I am sincerely grateful. Most of the stories which I read are not published in this book. There were just more stories than I had space. All of you, whether in this book or not, inspired the idea for this unique book. By your beautifully written insights into your emotions and thoughts about menstruation, you became the teacher and I the student. Thank you.

Following are the actual names of the individuals whose stories are in this book. All of their stories were written to be confidential, then each individual gave permission to publish. The names are listed in alphabetical order, not as their stories appear in the book: Carol Crnic, Tom DeCarlo, Susan Dutra, Heather Gillooly, Josephine Huber, Briana Johnson, Cara Johnson, Amy Karlstrom, Suzzane Kelleher, Jennifer Ko, Robert Lee, Sylvia Leick, Antonio Lopez Jr., Daniel Martin, Sian Leong-Nichols, Ingrid Muller, Janie Neal, Gregory Parrillo, Heidi Oljnik, Shelby Peak, Sonia Rahmati, Josephine Ragusa, Sydney Schaub, Ann Lythans Standby, Michelle Verkh, Elena White, Elizabeth Wood, Wendy Woodall, Jim Woodhead, and Julie Woodhead.

I wish to acknowledge the individuals who critically read the manuscript and gave their valuable comments and direction: Kim Bader, M.D., Maggie Freed, Carol Glazer, Kathy Kobayashi, Cindy Rose, Denise Seider, Lindsay Sipple, Sharon Sipple, Jefferson C. Stephens, Jr., Pamela Wald, M.D., Carol Walker, M.D., Gail Wetmore, Cynthia Whitham, MSW, and Connie Woodhead.

Special acknowledgment and thanks to Laura Golden Bellotti, editor of the manuscript. Your talent, intuition, and ability to understand what I was trying to say and help me say it clearly are remarkable. For Jean Barbaro, typist, who joined this team when it was time to "get it typed and done," thank you.

I treasure my mother and father's continued acceptance of my various projects and their many caring ways to help with my family responsibilities which allowed me to write. With gratitude I thank two extraordinary friends, Kathryn Gentry and Bart Edelman, who were always there to provide emotional support and wise guidance throughout each step of the process.

Contents

Introduction

During the writing of this book, I rarely found a woman who did not remember her first menstruation. This includes my grandmother who is 101 years old. I only had to mention that I was writing about menstruation, and she would share her personal story with me. Women are ready to tell their personal stories about menstruation, for it is our stories which connect us.

When talking with young girls, they were at first reluctant to share their stories but with a little encouragement, they told their feelings of beginning their periods. To my surprise, the stories of girls and women of all ages had one common theme: they needed more information about menstruation before they began their first periods. Even girls who acted as if they did not want or need conversations about their approaching menstruation, in fact later realized how valuable these conversations were. The more accurate the information they obtained, the fewer fears and anxieties they experienced.

The best way for your daughter to look forward with confidence to the day she begins her period is to begin your conversations with her while she is still young. You can reduce her fears and anxieties and bolster her self-confidence and acceptance of her maturing body by open discussions on the wonders of maturation and menstruation. Many parents have more trouble discussing the emotions that accompany menstruation than the physical changes, but our young daughters desperately need both the description of the physical changes and emotional guidance from us.

You will be well-prepared for these tasks if you read the chapters with their stories and do at least some of the suggested Things to Do and Things to Think About. If you have already started your talks about menstruation, this book will provide additional activities and suggestions to keep you talking. If you have not yet begun your talks, then this book will help you get started. For now is the time to begin talking with your daughter.

There is another reason to begin your talks while your daughter is still young. It is these early talks about menstruation which nourish communication between you and your daughter. Your talks with your young daughter about the physical and emotional aspects of menstruation prepare both of you for the more mature and sensitive topics which follow, such as dating, falling in love, being hurt by love, and expressing one's sexuality.

If you think your daughter is too young to start talking about menstruation, you may want to reassess. Preparing your young daughter could save her a lot of anxiety:

"I Didn't Think It Was Supposed to Happen to Little Girls" • Rebecca, Age 21

Before age ten, I thought menstruation was something that my mother had, like a disease or a condition. I knew that I would get this thing later so that I could have babies. My parents never discussed menstruation with me and I never asked about it. I believed that women did not get this until they were married.

However, during the summer of my tenth year, my whole concept of menstruation changed. My best friend, Sharon, who was nine at the time, had come over to swim at my house. After we finished swimming, we were sitting on my bedroom floor in our bathing suits playing Monopoly. Sharon got up for some reason. When she did there was a dark stain of blood on my floor where she had been sitting. We were both silent at first. Then I became very frightened and began to cry and call for my mother. I knew what a period was but I had no idea of how it would look. I certainly didn't think it was supposed to happen to little girls who were only nine.

Sharon became calm when my mother came. She stayed calm through the whole ordeal. When her parents came to get her, she ran and excitedly told her mother. Sharon's parents must have discussed menstruation with her so that she was prepared for it.

My parents were shocked that a nine year old could have her period. They were sorry that they had not given me any information about menstruation. Later that day, my mother told me a few general things about menstruation. I remember that she was uncomfortable as she gave me a basic description. I know that she thought she had at least two more years to prepare to tell me about periods. Sharon's experience rushed her. I also felt uncomfortable with the conversation. I felt a bit confused too. I forgot to ask her questions.

The next day I saw Sharon again and asked, "Do you feel any different?" She just gave me a funny look and said, "Why, should I?" I looked at her and realized that she had this "thing" that made her a woman. I knew that now she had the ability to make babies. Certainly, Sharon and I didn't know how to make babies but we were sure that this "thing" had something to do with it. I wanted it too!

This experience with Sharon was a major turning point in my own development. From that day on and for the next three years, I had this new awareness about menstruation. Every commercial seemed to be for some brand of sanitary napkin. It seemed that each time I turned around one of my friends was getting her period. I also began reading books by Judy Blume which talked about girls going into stores to buy sanitary pads for the first time, plus other menstruation stories. I began to want my period very badly. I remember feeling left out when the other girls would talk about what brand of tampon they used. It seemed that I was the last girl left on earth who didn't have a period yet.

I finally got my period when I was thirteen-and-a-half. I was at Magic Mountain Amusement Park wearing white pants, of course. I just walked off the Revolution ride and into a bathroom. There it was! I didn't have anything but some napkins. I quickly stuffed them into my panties. I didn't really care. I now had my period! I felt like some big weight had been lifted from my shoulders and that I had finally become a woman.

Rebecca's story points out the contrast between being well prepared for the onset of menstruation, and not being prepared. Sharon, whose parents had openly discussed with her what to expect physically and emotionally, was not upset on the day she got her first period. The fact that she was only nine years old yet took it all in stride meant that her parents probably began talking with her when she was about eight. Rebecca, on the other hand, was upset by her friend's first period because her own mother had not yet spoken to her about menstruation. Rebecca had only a vague idea concerning what the process was all about and when she might expect to get her first period.

Rebecca's mother, like many mothers today, hadn't realized how much younger girls are maturing these days, and that they therefore need to be given information about their changing bodies much sooner than girls in past generations. Even if, like Rebecca, your daughter doesn't get her period until she's twelve or thirteen, she will have heard about menstruation much earlier—through the media and her friends—and will begin to wonder about it. Her wonder may turn to worry unless you can speak openly with her and help to allay any fears she may have.

After reading hundreds of stories like Rebecca's, conducting workshops, and talking with mothers, fathers, and young girls, it became clear that young girls want to know more about menstruation. Parents, however, must actively take the lead, because most girls between the ages of seven and fourteen are excited, yet embarrassed, about this aspect of growing up.

Section I

Start Preparing

Girls today get their periods earlier than ever before. Are you ready to talk to your daughter? Despite the many pamphlets, books, and school health courses available, girls need their parents, and particularly their mothers, to talk to, to answer questions, and to offer support. It will be easier to talk with your daughter if you can remember how you felt.

Chapter 1

If your daughter is eight, she's old enough for the talks to begin

Mothers need to begin conversations about maturation, changing bodies, and menstruation when daughters are around eight years old. "But, why so young?" I am often asked. Daughters this age are still little girls. If your daughter's body has not begun to mature, it is difficult to believe that you need to get ready to talk with her. It is hard to imagine that her body will be mature anytime soon or that she will need to know anything about menstruation for many years to come. Yet, if she is between eight and ten years of age, her body is already beginning to mature. A hormone from her pituitary gland is being released into her blood supply while she sleeps. This process of physical maturity begins with internal changes before you notice any external differences. Before you know it, your little girl will reach puberty.

In the United States, children have been growing larger and maturing earlier since the beginning of the 1900s. In the past one hundred years, the average age of a girl's first menstrual cycle has decreased from approximately fourteen years to an average of twelve years. Currently some girls as young as nine or ten begin their normal menstrual cycle. Even though boys do not have such an outward sign of sexual maturity as menstruation, it is reasonable to assume that boys are also reaching their sexual maturity earlier than previous generations.

The April 1997 issue of *Pediatrics,* a journal published by the American Academy of Pediatrics, reported a study which analyzed average ages of onset of pubertal body changes in 17,077 young girls in the United States. Approximately 10 percent of the girls were African-American and 90 percent were white. The researchers concluded that: 1) the average age of the first menstrual period occurred at approximately 12 years of age for African-American girls and 12 years 8 months of age for white girls, 2) the average age of breast development was 8 years 8 months for African-American girls and 9 years 10 months for white girls, and 3) girls across the United States are developing pubertal characteristics at younger ages than previously thought. In fact, breast development or pubic hair growth was found in 3 percent of African-American girls and 1 percent of white girls at age 3 in this study. This finding came as a surprise to most people and was reported on radio and television programs across the United States.

No one is absolutely certain why children are maturing younger. The most accepted theory is that improved health care has increased children's weight and speeded up their growth rate. Prenatal and postnatal vitamins, enriched foods such as milk and bread, and overall improved nutrition and health care contribute to increased body weight. Genetics also play a part in the onset of adolescence.

Interestingly, girls who live in warm climates begin their periods earlier than girls who live in colder ones. This suggests that it is the warm weather or increased exposure to sunlight that initiates earlier growth and menstruation. Some theorists even believe that exposure to light (including electric light) is the reason that girls presently reach adolescence earlier than their great-great grandmother's generations. Regardless of the causes of accelerated maturation, it is clear that mothers need to prepare to talk with their daughters earlier than they might realize.

Following are six stories written by girls aged eight to fourteen who are waiting for their first periods. Each one of these stories was chosen because it addresses the typical questions, feelings, and concerns of young girls. These girls have previously received some information about menstruation as well as sanitary supplies. Their stories are impressive because the girls accurately connect their physical and emotional changes to their approaching menstruation. They are aware that their breast development, body changes, and unpredictable moods are a part of growing up. Yet they write about a common fear, a fear of the unknown. They may know what to do when their periods come, but they aren't certain how to deal with or interpret the emotions and feelings that come with menstruation.

These young girls' writings give many clues to why it is important to talk with your daughter as she waits for the unknown to happen. Before a girl gets her period for the first time, she has usually heard something about menstruation, but what she's heard from friends or what she has gleaned from television ads isn't always accurate. If your daughter is about eight years old, she has probably begun to be curious about this mysterious subject but may not know how to ask the right questions. Once you read the following stories describing the bewilderment, fears, frustrations, and anticipation experienced by young girls, you'll be much more apt to begin talking about menstruation with your daughter and to answer her unasked questions.

These stories can thus become ice breakers for conversations between the two of you. I find that young girls do not always immediately admit to their feelings of fear or confusion about menstruation, but if you begin by discussing the stories in this chapter and talking about how these girls felt, your daughter will feel more comfortable about the subject...and so will you.

I recommend that you read the stories twice. These stories are short and easy to read. The first time pay attention to the girls in the stories. Think about what they know, what they think they know, and what their anxieties and concerns are. The second time focus on the role of their mothers. Consider how the girls in these stories seek out their mother's guidance and reassurance.

Girls Waiting for Their First Periods

"Embarrassing" • Madaline, Age 11

Well, to start, waiting for "it" is easy and hard. It's easy because I don't want "it" that badly. I mean, sometimes, to me it's just a little extra thing that really doesn't need to happen. But it does. You couldn't have any kids without it. Sometimes, I feel anxious to get "it." Like I kind of want it. Only a few girls in the sixth grade have it. Most of the time it feels like a big hassle.

And what if you get "it" in the middle of social studies class? I mean, you just kind of notice that "it's" there. What then? For me, it would be the most embarrassing thing to have happen.

Wearing this pillow-thing in your underwear would be really uncomfortable. Or, even worse, something up your you-know-what.

But in the other sense, I kind of want it because it's like you are really growing up, you are a teenager. For me, I really want to be a teenager, learning to drive, having boyfriends and stuff like that.

Anyway, my mom tells me most of the stuff I know about it. She had to teach it so she is pretty open about it. Sometimes, I think in one sense that it's not fair. I mean, it's not like boys have to go through any of it. They hardly have to do anything. Of course, I'm not a boy. But still, it doesn't seem fair to me. And I'm only eleven. I won't be twelve until July. A lot of other girls are much more likely to get it than I am.

Just a couple of days ago, when I was in the girl's bathroom, I saw the paper part of the pad (what's left when you pull it off) on the floor. It said, "Beltless Maxis" or something like that. Of course, I knew right away what it was. But for the rest of the day I wondered whether it belonged to a teacher or a girl.

Last year there was this girl in my class who was twelve. She had her period. She carried tampons around in this weird, ugly purse. She carried it everywhere. The problem was that everyone knew she had her period. She didn't know that everyone knew, though. She thought it was a secret but it wasn't. I mean I don't want to be like that. I don't want the whole school to know when I get it. That about sums it up.

"I Don't Think About It Much" • Alissa, Age 12

I don't really think about menstruation much. Every once in a while it crosses my mind. I am definitely not looking forward to it. I do sort of wonder what it's like. I kinda worry about how it will affect the stuff I do and how I do it.

My mom says it's no big deal. But I don't know. My mom is the one who mainly tells me what I know about menstruation. I guess it is different for everyone. My friend's mom complains and sometimes even gets all mad for no reason in front of us. My mom doesn't get affected by menstruation hardly at all.

As for what I think about it, I really don't know. Like I said, I don't think about it a lot. So, I can't say a lot about it. It is really embarrassing to talk about it, though, especially like in class and stuff. I don't feel that it's a big problem for some reason. I understand it okay. I sometimes sort of ask myself questions like, "What's it like?" "What really happens?" "Why does it have to happen?" "What changes happen when it starts?", and stuff like that.

Thinking about menstruation is interesting though, isn't it? I'm not trying to be gross or anything. It's kind of weird and usually I don't even know what to think of it. I'm nervous about when I will start my period. What if I'm in school or something? And how am I supposed to tell my mom? What about my dad? Oh well, everyone goes through it so I might as well be positive and I'm sure I'll survive!! (Ha! Ha!)

"I Kind of Liked the Idea That I Was Growing Up" • Emily, Age 12

I got a lot of information about menstruation from school. I learned about all of the stages young women go through before entering adulthood. It scared me a bit to discover that my breasts would get larger and that I'd start growing hair other places besides my head. I talked with my mom about how my chest had started to get bigger. She told me I was getting ready to menstruate and grow into a young woman.

I kind of liked the idea that I was growing up. I was embarrassed at school. I always wore baggy shirts. But then I realized I wasn't the only one whose breasts were getting bigger. Many other girls were getting larger breasts, too.

I got very interested in menstruation. I read books about menstruation. The books were a lot more helpful and more exact than my friends. Now, I'm not saying that I don't go to my friends for answers. Just that I found a book more accurate. I found that my mom and my grandma are the best ones to ask. I can tell them my feelings about menstruation, too.

My mom got some sanitary napkins or pads for me. I tried one on and it kind of felt uncomfortable. I guess my mom could wear pads with no problem.

At school in P.E. I used to sweat a lot. I mean I just dripped sweat. I know that sounds gross but it is true. I thought maybe there was something wrong with me. I am perfectly healthy. I just happen to sweat more than others.

One night I was getting ready for my bath and I discovered some yellowish-clear stuff on my underwear. My mom said not to worry. It was just some stuff from my body. I feel kind of anxious for my period to come. I don't know why but I just do.

"Half of Me Says, 'I Can Hardly Wait,' and the Other Half Says, 'Bummer'" • Noelle, Age 12

I feel I'm waiting very patiently for my period. When I think about it, half of me says, "I can hardly wait." The other half says, "Bummer." A couple of good things about menstruation is that I can have babies, experience having a cycle, and be able to wear neat pads. Some bad things are those "neat pads" may not be so comfy. It might be a hassle to deal with every month. I also worry about cramps.

Some things I know about menstruation are that between the ages of nine and nineteen a girl will find blood on her underwear. The blood is the lining of the uterus where an egg would be stored if it were fertilized. This blood comes every so often and needs to be soaked up so it doesn't ruin a lot of underwear.

Sometimes, I don't think it's fair that boys don't have their periods, too. A couple of books that have influenced me are: *Are You There God?, It's Me Margaret*, and *How Does My Body Work, A Book for Girls*. A few people who have influenced me in learning about menstruation are my friends, my parents, and friends of my parents.

Sometimes, I'm scared my period will affect me when we go camping, what pants I should wear to school and what boys will think. I'm also scared to ask a male or female teacher to go to the bathroom during instruction.

A few things I don't really understand about menstruation are why do girls change to women, and why isn't there a sign that says, "It's coming, get ready." A fun thing I've found with menstruation is that if you put a tampon in water it puffs out.

I hope my period comes on a regular basis. I think it would be hard to judge when to have a baby if it didn't come on a regular basis. I worry about when my period will come because I think when I get my period I'm not going to like it.

One thing that is hard for me is getting used to wearing bras and different sized underwear.

One thing I will never forget is when my guinea pig, Squeaker, was alive, I thought she would get her period, too. My dad told me that animals have a period of time when they are in heat. I told him that maybe we should buy our next guinea pig in the winter time. He then explained that "in heat" meant that a female animal was able to produce an egg and that's when a female guinea pig could get pregnant. So, I can buy my new guinea pig in summer or winter and she can get to be "in heat." I'm shy and excited about my period. I hope it will be an important time in my life.

"Physical and Mental Maturity are Different" • Sarah, Age 14

I am in eighth grade, but I still don't have my period. That really doesn't bother me. It might bother someone else. I don't see it as something to be proud of or upset about, nor as an excuse of any kind. I don't expect my life to change after getting my period.

My earliest memory about menstruation is just my mom telling me about it when I was little, maybe six or seven years old. It's something that my mom has been very open about, and I've never been embarrassed about it.

I don't like to tell people that I don't have my period because they assume that because I am 14, I definitely have it. Often people who don't know any better will use menstruation as a measure of maturity. It is a measure of physical maturity. Physical maturity is something I have no control over—something no one has control over yet.

Often people will regard a young lady who has not yet gotten her period as mentally immature. That is wrong. I have no control over when I will get my period. I consider myself lucky that I don't have to deal with it. To me, menstruation is like eating or breathing. It's a fact of life. But it's a part of life for young ladies that they cannot control—so do not consider yourself inferior to anyone else, if you don't have your period—I don't.

My friends, most of them, do menstruate. At first, I was looked down upon because I did not. But, that was short-lived and my friends realized that it was nothing to be proud or ashamed of. In the beginning (when my friends first got their periods), they were very proud of it. Also, they would complain to me about it. They realized that I couldn't say anything to them because I didn't know how they felt. When I do get my period, I will not be proud or ashamed. I will not complain. It's one of those things—period.

"Little Dots" • Annette, Age 8

I first learned about menstruation when I was reading a paper my friend was writing about her period. I thought it meant that little dots would grow on you. I have learned that isn't true. I asked my mother to tell me about periods. She told me and I said, "Yuck!"

My best friend, who is twelve, got her period and she was happy. She called to tell my mother and me about her special day.

I am only eight years old and my body has not started to change. Some of the girls in my grade have started to develop in certain parts. These girls all weigh more than I do and I do not mind it so far. The girls who have started to develop talk more about boys than I do for some reason. All us girls get along well and play together the same as always.

As you can tell young girls are aware and think about menstruation. After completing the Things To Do and Things To Think About, you will be ready to prepare your young daughter for menstruation.

Things To Do

- Write down how you think your daughter will feel (or does feel) about her changing body, menstruation, and growing up. Will she have similar feelings to any of these girls? If so, which one or ones?

- Write down what you think your daughter already knows about menstruation. After you begin your talks, check out if she really knows what you think she does.

Things to Think About

- The girls wrote that their mothers were important sources of information for them. Was your mother your major source of information about menstruation? If not, who (or what) was?

- Do you remember your desire to have your mother or loved-one talk with you about menstruation?

- Did you go through a period of waiting for menstruation, or did you start before your friends? What was this experience like for you?

- What do you think the girls in the stories still need to know before they begin to menstruate?

- Are your daughter's moods or emotions presently changing? If so, might these changes be the beginning of puberty?

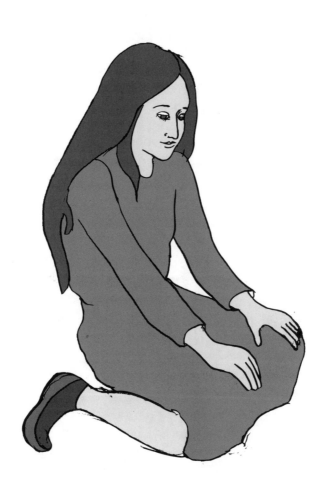

Chapter 2

Can you remember
your first period?

The purpose of this chapter is to help you remember your first time and evaluate your own feelings about menstruation so that you'll be better prepared to talk with your daughter about what she can expect. Mothers want their daughters to make the transition into menstruation with as little fear, shame and embarrassment as possible, but they often recall having experienced one or more of these negative feelings when they were younger. Some mothers remember feeling ashamed because they didn't know all the facts about menstruation when they were young—and recall getting teased about their ignorance by other girls (or boys). Many women remember either their own embarrassing girlhood "accidents" during school or social occasions, or those of other girls—which filled them with the fear that this could happen to them. And most of us have felt the anxiety associated with starting our period at the wrong time (our wedding day, for example). With such negative memories, how can we communicate to our daughters that menstruation is a normal, healthy body function that can be anticipated with confidence and a positive outlook?

Once you have taken the time to reassess your own early menstruation experiences—either positive or negative—you'll have a clearer idea of how to prevent the misinformation and negativity you may have received. And you will have a good idea how to pass along the reassurance and helpfulness that you want your daughter to feel from you.

One very important activity is to write your own story of menstruation. This will give you clarity about what went on in your life as well as more confidence in helping your daughter grasp the meaning of her own menstruation story. Some women find it difficult to write their stories because they have never thought that their memories concerning menstruation were important. When researching women's life stories, Wanda Johnson, Ph.D., a colleague of mine, found that most women did not include their menarche (MEN-arc-kee), first menstrual period, as part of their life stories. When questioned, these women readily admitted that menstruation had played an important part in their lives. Yet it had not occurred to them to talk about menstruation as a significant event.

In some cultures mothers pass on to their daughters the personal stories of the women in their immediate families. Many mothers tell their own mother's personal story, which reduces the embarrassment of talking about themselves. Daughters thus have the stories of their grandmothers, the observations of their mothers, and their own experiences to draw on to understand their own menstruation.

If you know the stories of your mother and other family members, include them when you write your own story. All these personal stories of menstruation are significant both to you and your daughter. Therefore, I encourage you to write.

For many women, their memory of menstruation is full of anticipation, closeness with family or friends, and lots of laughter. For others, their memory holds feelings of shame, embarrassment, and ignorance. No one likes uncomfortable memories, and such discomfort makes writing personal stories more difficult. However, writing is an excellent way to reassess our memories, and to examine them from a more mature vantage point. Also by getting in touch with your past feelings and experiences, you will be more sensitive to what your daughter might be feeling.

If your childhood or sexual experiences included sexual abuse, physical abuse, illness, infertility, or surgery connected to your reproductive organs, your memories may not be pleasant ones. Any one of these events makes it more difficult to feel open and communicative with your daughter about menstruation. As you begin to write about your personal history, you may want to talk with a counselor, friend, spouse, or partner about these uncomfortable experiences. You may find that seeking professional help from a Marriage, Family, and Child Counselor or a psychologist who specializes in women's issues would be helpful. I encourage you to write, even if it is difficult, because it can be a part of the healing process. Writing and talking are powerful ways to clarify and heal past hurts and wounds.

Here are two stories to help you remember some of your own early menstrual experiences. The beauty of these stories is in how these women blend humorous accounts of their experiences, with serious aspects of menstruation.

Remembering

"Never Wear White Pants" • Tina, Age 31

We had spent a week of our summer vacation at Big Bear Lake and now we were at Lake Havasu, a furnace in the August heat. I, being only ten years old, was immune to the temperature and spent every minute in the water. I hardly noticed that my mother wasn't sitting on the shore watching me as she usually did. She had spent the entire day inside the camper. The realization of her absence came when my father announced that we would be leaving for home the next day because Mom wasn't feeling well. Angry that my summer paradise was being pulled out from under me, I demanded to know the reason for this outrageous decision. My father, either embarrassed by my question or simply responding from habit replied, "Ask your mother."

Mom, with a pained look on her face, explained to me that she was having her period and that the combination of the heat and the cramps was simply unbearable. I knew what a woman's period was, although I don't remember exactly the year I learned this. I also had been warned about cramps. However, I didn't know that they could so disrupt one's life as to shorten a marvelous vacation. In fact, I was convinced that my mother was faking it. She never did like the hot desert!

Although I don't remember exactly when my mother told me about menstruation, I do remember some of the things she said. She explained that once a month my body would soon start making a nest for an egg that would travel from my ovary to my uterus. The nest was a place where the egg, if fertilized by a sperm, could grow into a baby. (Since I already knew about sexual intercourse, I didn't need her to repeat those details about the egg and sperm meeting. They were enough of a shock the first time around!)

Mom said that if the egg was not fertilized, the egg and nest would be shed. This shedding process took about a week to complete, and during that time I would need to wear a Kotex pad to catch the bloody "nest." It all sounded weird and messy to me, not to mention being confused by her choice of words: "egg," which I visualized as the kind we scrambled for breakfast; "fertilize," which was what we did to our lawn with Bat Guano, and "shed," which was what a snake did with its skin. My first thought was that this icky process might happen to some girls, but it would certainly not happen to me.

When I was in sixth grade, all the girls my age and their mothers were invited to a special meeting in the cafeteria. I was excited about spending this special time with my mom, and thought it was going to be like a party with entertainment and refreshments. Much to my disappointment, it was a presentation given by a nurse about our changing bodies. My mother had already filled me in on most of the details but I was aware that the nurse had a much different attitude about menstruation than did my mom. The nurse was much more positive than my mom had been. She emphasized that our periods should not interfere with our normal lives. She said we should continue sports and all the activities we enjoyed, as long as we felt up to it.

When my mom first explained to me about menstruation, she had gone on at great length about her miserable cramps, the headaches she had and how she, in her teen years, had spent at least one day a month in bed with a hot water bottle. The impression made on me by my mom and her story of menstruation had a much greater impact than the story told by the school nurse.

Bass Lake was our destination the following summer. One afternoon, as I was changing into my bathing suit, it happened. I pulled down my underpants and there it was—blood! It had happened to me! I felt a combination of fear, joy, excitement, and pride that I was a woman. Well, I didn't really think of myself as a woman. Mom had said that when a girl started her period it meant that she could get pregnant, so I guessed that I qualified as a woman. I had started before any of my friends, (I was eleven), so that gave me an extra thrill. Then Mom told Dad. I wanted to die. The man who hadn't even been able to tell me why Mom had been so sick the summer before now knew that this "thing" had happened to me. My father had always had little contact with me. At that moment, as I stood on the threshold of womanhood, I remember thinking, "Now he'll never want to have anything to do with me."

Seventh grade brought many new experiences; among them was gym class. I hated having to change my clothes in front of other girls and, even worse, showering in front of them. Thanks to Mom, however, I knew just what buttons to push and pretended menstrual cramps whenever possible. Since Mom's own experience had been so negative, she never once questioned whether or not I was truly in pain. She gladly wrote many notes to excuse me from P.E. and even entire days of school. I had struck gold! I prayed that my period would be at the same time as whichever test I was dreading the most. I received the royal treatment at home. I especially enjoyed the hot water bottle and meals in bed.

Sitting in the hay wagon with knees wide open and wearing white pants, my friend, Sandy, had the misfortune of her tampon leaking. To add to her misery, it was a boy who informed her of the fact. I was determined to never let such an incident occur in my life.

It did! I had been attending Sunday School at my friend Judy's church. Judy, you must understand, was perfect—I wondered why she even needed church. Unlike Sandy, Judy never approached the subject of sex—or any other body function, for that matter. One Sunday morning, I had the audacity to wear my black mini-skirt to church (probably just to raise Judy's eyebrows). As fate would have it, or maybe it was the wrath of God for my irreverent skirt, I started my period. Our Sunday school class finished. I rose from my folding chair and turned to put it away. I was horrified by the puddle of blood on the seat. I quickly collapsed my chair and looked to see if it had been noticed. It had not. Due to the fear of being found out, it never occurred to me to clean up the mess in the chair. I had to get home to clean myself and put on a Kotex.

Since Judy expected me to go on into the main service with her, I was forced to tell her that I had started my period, and that I would call my mom to come and get me. She looked at me as if I were an extraterrestrial! I was convinced that Judy was too good to have periods. I kept my courage and returned with Judy the following Sunday. As we were unfolding the chairs, an unfortunate girl came across my former chair. All heads turned her way at the cry of, "Yuck, what's this?" She exposed the brown blood stain. I remained silent. The class started and the chair was forgotten. If Judy put the evidence together and knew I had caused the stain, she never said anything to me. I learned to be more careful about wearing mini-skirts and to never wear one to church.

At the tender age of seven weeks, I had to have an ovary removed. I got gangrene from having a strangulated hernia. Because of this, my periods have never been regular. When I decided to marry at the age of nineteen, I could not, as most women try to do, time my wedding to avoid having my period then. I was due any day at the time of my marriage, and I was afraid that I would start on my wedding day while dressed in white.

Fortunately, my period did not start then. In fact, it was missed entirely as I became pregnant immediately—perhaps on our wedding night. I miscarried that pregnancy. I later had two beautiful, healthy children.

"Dear Diary: Last Night I Got It!" • Teresa, Age 20

It all started when I was in fifth grade. It was picture day at school. That morning, I picked my favorite dress and let my long hair down instead of my usual pig tails or braids. In class, I sat by my best friend, Monica, who suddenly started giggling uncontrollably and whispering to the girl next to her. Later that day, I found the reason for her laughter. I was getting boobs. They were not big or anything, just two barely noticeable bumps on my chest. Monica had noticed them and found them very funny. I was embarrassed by her teasing. The teasing soon came to an abrupt end for Monica started getting boobs, also. This was an awkward time for me. I was excited about getting a womanly figure, yet I was frightened and embarrassed by all the teasing that was going on.

By the time sixth grade came around a number of the girls in my class were getting breasts, so having them was becoming more accepted. We started being proud of our newly acquired figures, and the girls without breasts were the ones getting teased. Like me, most of the girls in the sixth grade had read, *Are You There God? It's Me Margaret*. This book, written by Judy Blume, was about a girl whose friends were all getting their periods and she wasn't getting hers yet. She was eager to get her period so she could be considered a young woman like all her friends and feel like one, too. By the end of the book, Margaret got her period and that was the happy ending.

Luckily for me on Friday night, March 30th, I got my period. I was relieved it had not come at school. My period was not what I expected it to be. There were just a few spots of blood on my panties. I didn't feel any cramps either. I immediately ran to the box of maxi pads that I had bought for this occasion. I put one on. I felt so proud. I went upstairs into my mom's room and asked her, "Guess what I got?" She guessed a few different things, and I kept saying, "No," with a big smile on my face. I had been giggling at her answers. Finally, in a very serious voice she said, "You got your period." Her tone of voice was not happy like mine was. She sounded more worried than anything else. I could tell that she was trying to be kind and supportive. I decided to ask my mom when she had gotten her period. She told me that she was sixteen years old. Here I was only twelve and getting my period. I never asked my mother why her voice sounded worried when I told her about my period, but I think that she was not prepared for me to begin my menarche so early.

The day after my period started, I began writing in a diary. I found it and here is what I wrote on the first couple of lines:

"Dear Diary,
    Today is so boring like most Saturdays are. Last night I got it!!! It wasn't bad like I heard it would be."

Anyway, then I went on to write about other extremely important matters such as boys. It was a turning point in my life. I was becoming a young lady. I am so happy that I started keeping my own diary. It gives me such joy to read back through those pages. I continue to write in my journal daily.

In the Spanish culture I grew up in, when a girl gets her period, she is no longer considered a little girl. She automatically becomes a young woman. To be a young woman at the age of twelve was a big responsibility for me. I knew that I was a little girl inside even though I had the beginnings of a womanish body on the outside. Attention from boys, even boys in high school, started to increase. I was flattered yet awkward with boys. I was trying to fit this new body and me together so that I could feel like one person again.

Hopefully, you enjoyed these stories, and they have helped you retrieve memories of your own early menstrual experiences, growing up and maturing. It is your ability to recall what it was like to be the young girl who was learning about menstruation that will help you to identify with your young daughter's attitudes towards growing up—and, consequently, better prepare her for her own menstrual experiences.

One common theme in Teresa's story is that her breasts developed earlier than her friends'. She was teased by girls and boys and felt embarrassed by her emerging breasts. Did you develop physically earlier than your classmates? Do you think that your daughter will be or is developing sooner than the other girls her age? If the answer is "yes," then you can anticipate that she likely will be teased. And, like most girls, she will feel embarrassed and awkward about her changing body. As you write your story, think back to feelings you had about your physical development.

Teresa's story gives insight into another common theme of menstruation. Even though many girls feel embarrassed about physically maturing, they are usually excited about starting their periods. Teresa wanted to share the good news with her mother. Did you want to tell your mother about beginning your period? Did you want her help and reassurance that everything was all right? Did you sense your mother's unspoken words about how she felt about you physically becoming a woman?

Tina and Teresa write about a daughter's close observation of their mother's spoken and unspoken language. Chances are that neither of these mothers believed that their underlying feelings of apprehension or surprise were recognized by their daughters. Do you remember your mother's reactions to your announcement that you had started your period? Did she seem genuinely happy for you? How did you want her to feel? How do you want to feel and be when your daughter tells you, "Guess what I got?"

Tina writes about her mother's cramps. Most girls hear about cramps and pain associated with menstruation. What did you know about cramps before you started your period? What have been your experiences?

Writing Your Own Story

As you think about how you have experienced menstruation throughout your life—from the time of your first period, through young adulthood, becoming sexually active, becoming a mother, to present feelings about menopause—you can use the following guidelines to write your own story.

- Do not worry about spelling, punctuation, etc. You are not writing to be published or graded. Your story is for you. It is your decision whether or not to show it to anyone else.

- Use the following questions to stir your memories and help you begin your story of menstruation:
  Where were you when you got your first period?
  How did it feel physically?
  How did you feel emotionally?
  How did you know that this was the beginning of menstruation?
  Was there anything surprising about this first time?
  With whom did you share the news that you had gotten your period for the first time?
  How did each member of your family react to the news of your maturity?

Did your relationship with mother, father, brother, sister, other relatives, change? How?

Who were the people who taught you the most about menstruation?

Who taught you how to use sanitary pads and tampons?

How did you feel when you first learned the facts about menstruation?

Who were the people who helped you develop a positive attitude about menstruation?

Who were the people who were NOT helpful in creating a positive attitude about menstruation?

What did you wish you knew, but no one told you?

How did you deal with your period when you were physically active—i.e., playing sports, camping, swimming, etc.?

As you got older, how did you tell the boys and men in your life about your menstrual needs and concerns?

How has menstruation influenced your sex life, if at all?

How have dieting, stress, childbirth, or surgery affected your period, if at all?

How do you feel about menopause and ending menstruation?

- Schedule 30 to 60 minutes to be alone, think and write.

- Ask your mother, sister, or friend to also write her story of menstruation and menopause. You can choose to share, either through conversations or reading each other's stories. I am always surprised at the energy, laughter, and excitement that women generate when talking about this uniquely female experience. Women's stories connect us from generation to generation.

Chapter 3

Our culture shapes our menstruation experiences

As you think about your own menstruation story, you may be tempted to criticize yourself for what you did not know and what you did not do. Don't. It is not your fault if no one told you about menstruation before your first period. Today, in our culture, we consider it important for a girl to know about menstruation before it happens. It is primarily the mother's job to inform, but pediatricians routinely ask young patients if they know about menstruation, and many elementary schools offer some menstruation education. A short time ago, though, doctors did not even ask, schools waited until junior high or high school, and many mothers felt that the best time for The Talk was when a girl started her period.

Did you ever wonder why you've never seen a collection of menstruation stories? After all, more than half of the adult population has such a story to tell. This silence has to do with the attitudes and behaviors toward menstruation that our society carries as norms. Although individuals may have their own beliefs about appropriate behavior, our middle class American society shares a sense of what is acceptable, important, embarrassing or shameful in every area of human conduct, including menstruation.

Society's Unwritten Rules about Menstruation

- Keep menstruation invisible.

- Never let males know when you are menstruating.

- Call materials used to catch the menstrual flow "sanitary supplies," creating the implication that women who use them are dirty. (You may also call them "feminine hygiene products," which still implies the same thing.)

- If you can't explain a woman's anger, blame it on menstruation.

- Menstrual flow has a terrible odor that needs to be covered up with douching or perfume.

- PMS (premenstrual syndrome) is blamed whenever women express their emotions or convictions.

- Menarche is not worthy of a public celebration.

- Boys don't need education about menstruation since it is irrelevant to them.

Even if you do not believe in them, some of their messages may have made you feel badly and might very well make your daughter feel badly about herself.

This brings us back to your own menstrual story. Think about how society's rules influenced your story.

For instance, you probably saw a movie at school when you were in the sixth, seventh, or eighth grade which was for girls only, no boys allowed. Do you remember seeing such a movie about menstruation and growing up in school? If so, how did you feel about seeing it: special, important, embarrassed, ashamed?

How did you cope after the movie? Did you tell the boys who were excluded from the movie what you saw?

What message does this separateness send to girls and to boys? Does it denote that there is something secret about females, something schools or society or parents don't want boys to know about girls? Or is it that boys don't need to know about female development and menstruation—it's a girl thing?

Many women say that the sexual revolution and women's liberation movements of the 1970's have changed a girl's or woman's ability to be more open about menstruation in general and around men in particular. Did these movements help you to feel more open? Do you talk more openly today on this subject than your mother or grandmothers did?

Advertisements for tampons and sanitary pads have become common place on television and in print media. Some of you no doubt remember when these menstrual supplies were not advertised as openly as they are today.

Have advertisements helped women and men become more communicative about menstruation? Have they helped society to be more responsive to females' needs in this area?

Have advertisements presented a clear picture of menstruation? Or have they added a new worry for females; for instance, the hygiene, odor-causing menstrual flow which must be masked with perfumed pads and products? Or have advertisements perpetuated the secretive aspect of menstruation while selling the products?

Here is a joke about a six-year-old boy who went to see his pediatrician for a check-up; the doctor, making conversation, asked him what he would buy if someone gave him five dollars:

"That's easy," replied Jim. "I would buy a Tampax." The doctor was surprised by his answer. "Why would you buy a Tampax?" "I don't know what it is exactly, but they say on TV that you can swim, ride horseback and even roller skate any time you want. That would certainly be worth five dollars."

As you read the following story, think about how your daughter's attitudes may be influenced by the times she lives in. Is she going to be open, proud or embarrassed and secretive about her menstruation? Have times changed, or not, for young girls?

Society's Influence

"I Still Want to Play With the Boys" • Farah, Age 20

It was a cold winter day. Our whole yard was covered with snow. I was really happy because I was having a great day at school. Now I was ready for my favorite lunch. I got home and threw my backpack next to my desk and hurried to the bathroom. Everyone was getting ready to have lunch. A few seconds later I heard my voice echo in the bathroom. "Mom," I was screaming. My mother came to me, looked at the blood stain on my pants, and said, "It's all right. It is nothing to worry about. Now you are a grown-up girl and this is your menstruation. You will have it every month, and I will now show you where I keep the pads." My mother then opened a drawer and handed me a pad. She showed me how to use it and left me alone with my thoughts in the bathroom. The pad was too thick, and I could neither comfortably stand nor sit. My whole appetite was gone and I just wanted to be left alone. In spite of the fact that I had friends who had already started their menstruation, my mother had talked about it with me, and we had had a special study for menstruation in my ballet class, it still came as a shock to me. I was thirteen when I started. I am now twenty and I still remember that day well. I remember how I hated myself and the whole world. I felt that this was an end of my freedom and happiness. I felt dirty. I had to change pads every two hours. The first month was horrible. The second was not as bad, and then I started accepting it and getting used to it.

After a year I started having bad cramps and a lot of pain. At that time, I refused to take pills and I wanted to fight my pain. That was a big mistake. There were days that the pain was so great that I had to be sent home from school in tears. Our neighbors could hear my cries. I was really miserable and kept to myself those days of the month. Plus, I did not want anybody to know about my menstrual time. For some reason, I was ashamed of menstruating.

My friends from ballet class were the first among my friends to find out about my menstruation. Their positive reaction made me feel somewhat better. I recall my English teacher, who was a role model for me, used to tell me that I was becoming a perfect woman, and I should be proud instead of being so ashamed of it. The only problem was that I had a strong negative attitude towards my menstruation, and it was not easy to turn this into a positive one.

I think that two main factors started this negative attitude. The first factor was the position of women in the society in Iran where I was born. The second reason was the cramps that I had. Perhaps a short description of my Iranian background can help explain part of my negative attitude toward my menstruation.

I was born in Tehran, the capital of Iran. I was seven years old when the revolution happened and the Islamic Republic of Iran was formed. My mother is a Christian who had immigrated from the Soviet Union to Iran many years ago. My father is a Moslem whose religion is the least of his interests. I used to spend a lot of time with my father. I also played in the street with boys. I liked the boys and wanted only to play with them and be like them. In order to take me out of my roughness, my mother enrolled me in ballet classes. There I found a lot of my best female friends. In Iran women are considered inferior to men. Their main job is to stay at home, take care of the children, and be their husband's slave. Definitely, their rights and problems are the least of concern.

All the women I knew, except my English teacher, were housewives. Iranian society does not accept women being divorced, not married, or independent in any way. Furthermore, after the revolution any relationship between boys and girls before marriage was forbidden according to the Islamic religion. I was, therefore, forced to stop seeing some of my closest friends because they were males. I was also going through these physical changes, including menstruation, which showed that I was becoming an older girl, and that meant losing my freedom and independence even more.

It was my dream to become a doctor and be on my own. To make my dream come true, I associated with boys because they were the ones who wanted to grow up to have careers. Their goal was not getting married and staying at home. When I lost contact with the boys, the members of my family became my only support and help in accomplishing my goals. Up to that time, I was raised to be responsible, outgoing and, most important of all, independent.

Suddenly I had to give up all my dreams and male friends—a change for what I considered the worst. As a result of the revolution, menstruation meant I was one step closer to becoming a typical Persian woman. This fear kept growing in me. After I started to menstruate, there was no one to whom I could talk about this at home. Therefore, positive reactions to my menstruation by my ballet friends were helpful. These girls came from more educated families and they had career goals. They were more open in their talk so I was able to tell them some of my feelings and fears. Talking about menstruation and life in general with them took a big weight off my shoulders. I soon stopped feeling so sorry for myself and looked at the matter from a totally different point of view.

The other factor that led me to my negative attitude toward menstruation was the cramps I had. The pain was too much for me. Sometimes I could not handle it. My mother would give me some pain killers. I refused them most of the time because I wanted to be strong and fight my pain. Nobody took me to a doctor because they thought that I was too young to see a gynecologist. In Iran women get married as a virgin so they do not consult a gynecologist before marriage.

I wish that I had consulted a doctor there. When I was a young adult, I finally consulted a gynecologist after I got to the United States. The doctor found a bloody cyst on my right ovary. This cyst had caused so much damage that I had to have that ovary removed. If the cyst had been noticed earlier, perhaps it could have been removed without losing one of my ovaries. I wish the Iranian beliefs about women and doctors were different. I do not want younger Iranian women to lose their ovaries because they cannot consult a doctor before marriage. I am happy that my family and close friends helped me to know that menstruation does not mean that I have to give up my future goals.

Things To Do

- Add to your menstruation story. Include your thoughts on how society influenced your story.

- Refer back to the list of Society's Unwritten Rules about Menstruation. Add to the list and make sure you include things specific to your own culture or religion.

- Go to the library and look through magazines for young girls and women. Notice the advertisements for feminine hygiene products. Consider the ads with these questions in mind: Does this educate my daughter about menstruation? Does it give specific instructions on how and where this product is to be used? Does it connect menstruation to having children? What is the appeal to make the product attractive?

- Pay attention to ads on television. If you did not know the purpose of the products, would you understand the advertisements? What do you think the ads are really selling?

- Discuss with other women how they might catch their menstrual flow if they could not buy anything from the feminine hygiene department. What did women do before they could by pads and tampons? How do women in third world countries deal with it today?

- Review the curriculum for menstruation education in your daughter's school. Pay special attention to how boys are taught about menstruation. Ask about equity in education.

- Make a list of instances in your life when menstruation was observed or discussed in public—i.e., observed on a girl's jeans or on a pad, referred to in an anecdote or joke, or discussed with pride. Consider how people responded. Was their response helpful or hurtful to women?

Things To Think About

- Does your religion have restrictions during menstruation? Does it have a celebration? What do you think of them?

- If you know women from different cultures, you might want to discuss their cultural views on menstruation. How are their views similar to yours? How are they different?

- When do you feel that you became a woman? Was it related to menstruation? If so, why? If not, why not?

Chapter 4

What is it like for young girls who have started their periods?

As you wrote your own menstruation story, you had the opportunity to think about the roles that your family, friends, society and the media have played in shaping your feelings and behavior. Now we are going to turn our attention to the experiences of girls today who have been menstruating for only a few years. Their stories reveal not only feelings of embarrassment, fear, and uncertainty, but also anticipation, excitement, and pride as the girls pass this milestone of female development. You will notice that these girls have learned more about their bodies than the girls in the waiting stage, and maybe more that you knew at their ages. They are willing to give advice and reassurance to those who are still waiting. Some of the information they have received about menstruation has come from school and friends, but the majority of the girls in this chapter credit their mothers with teaching them what they most needed and wanted to know.

Perhaps, like many other mothers, you think you're not as well-prepared to teach your daughter as professional teachers, nurses or physicians. But professionals have their limitations. Teachers in public and private schools can only teach what has been approved by their school boards, and school policies don't take into account your daughter's personality or your family's values. Physicians and nurses often do not have time to explain fully and your daughter may be shy about asking questions. Although professionals may do an excellent job explaining biology and hygiene, they may not adequately address a young girl's emotional issues. Your knowledge of your daughter's personality, your desire to teach your family's values, and your love for your daughter mean that you are the only one who can play this uniquely important role in her education on this subject.

Your daughter may one day feel like Sonia, a young girl whose story you will read in this chapter. She writes: "I feel that menstruation is a key that unlocks a whole new world of growing up." Her observation reinforces how crucial menstruation is to a young girl's understanding of what it means to grow up. A girl's need for both accurate information and access to her mother for ongoing dialogues cannot be overemphasized. You are a very important piece of the key that unlocks for your daughter the fascinating process of female development.

As you read the following stories, think about which girl's attitude about discussions on menstruation is most similar to your daughter's. These stories were chosen because together they present the most often expressed concerns and feelings of young girls' fears and yearnings about menstruation. Since these girls have been menstruating for about two years, they remember how they felt before and right after menstruation. They are clear in what they thought they wanted before menstruation, but realize that they needed their mothers' input and ongoing dialogues more than they originally imagined.

First Period

"I'd Rather Be Fishing" • Ellen, Age 14

I started my period when I was 12 years old. My mother tried to talk with me about menstruation before I started. I was about 10 or 11 then, but I wasn't interested and I put her off. I'd say things like, "Oh, Mom, that's so disgusting. I don't want to talk about it." Then I'd walk away. My mother was determined. About six months later she tried again, but I still didn't want to hear about it. I didn't think that I needed to hear about it. What I knew about it grossed me out. And I certainly didn't want to talk about menstruation with my mother!

My mother left me alone for awhile and then she gave me books about physical changes of girls and boys during adolescence. I was a bit more interested, but still not much. So what does my mother do? She brings the books about menstruation and maturing with us on our summer vacation! One afternoon when my father and brother were out fishing, my mother says, "Let's have a nice day together." Her idea of a nice day was sitting in the cabin with her reading out loud to me about my changing body. UGH!!! Awful—Terrible—It was a long day! I wanted to be anywhere but there, even fishing, and I hate fishing. I did learn many things that day about menstruation and my body. And, of course, my mother did talk about it even when I wasn't interested, which I wasn't.

When I did start my period, I was glad that she had talked with me about menstruation. I started my period at home. I simply went to the bathroom, and when I wiped it was right there. Perfect timing for once in my life. I knew what was happening because mother had tried so hard to educate me. I went looking for mother. I said, "I think I got it." Thank goodness my mother didn't make a big deal of it. She was more matter of fact. She took me to the bathroom and showed me where the pads were kept. She told me how to use one and left me alone with the pads.

I didn't have cramps or any problems in the beginning and I still don't. I know when my periods are coming. In the mornings, my stomach feels kind of funny, and by afternoon I start my period. I've learned what that funny feeling means. It is not pains or cramps. Now, I mark my calendar with little "x's" when I have my period. It comes one time a month for five days. Days 1 and 2 are my heavier flow days; day 3 lighter; day 4 I skip, and Day 5 I flow lightly. It took me a while to catch on to how my body menstruates and that 4th day is tricky.

I was the first one in my class to begin my period, as far as I know. Now, my friends and I talk about it, and they are all menstruating at 14 years old. We have an ongoing argument about the use of tampons. Some of us think tampons are uncomfortable and disgusting. Just the thought of putting something up inside your body, your vagina, sounds horrible. Other friends of mine, including myself, feel that they couldn't live without tampons. If my friends and I don't want someone, especially boys, to know what we're talking about, then we call our periods, "OTR." OTR stands for, "on the rag."

Physically and mentally maturing are hard times in life. It's scary and a gross out time. Today, when I start my period, I'm not happy. When it ends, I am. But I don't dread it. I don't think about it other times during the month. Luckily, no one said to me, "You've become a woman!" I didn't feel like I had become a woman. Today at 14, I feel like I am becoming more and more like a woman. I don't feel like my life changed when I started my period. I just see it as a part of growing up. It is something all woman have to go through. It's cool that I could create a life now, but I'd never choose to at this point in my life.

I have a 12 year old brother who is unclear about the whole subject of menstruation. He doesn't talk to me about it, and I don't talk to him. My father would talk to me about menstruation, but I don't like to discuss it with him. He doesn't ask me about it, since he knows that I don't want to discuss this with him. I just don't talk to boys or my father about these things. If I need information, I go ask my mother. I think that my mother and father talk about my maturing, but that doesn't bother me. As long as I don't have to talk a lot about menstruation, that suits me just fine.

"I Don't Want a Party" • Sarita, Age 13

Before I had my period, I was worried about three things. First, I was afraid people would notice that I had my period. Secondly, I was afraid of pain. I had seen my older half-sister lie on the couch not wanting to get up when she had her period. Lastly, I was afraid that my mother would actually carry out her threat that she would throw a party for me when I had it.

When my mother first started talking about menstruation, I was really worried that one day I'd go to the bathroom and my pants would be all bloody. I got so tired of being worried that I wished my period would come soon. When I was eleven, I came home from horseback riding. I went to the bathroom and there was a little blood on my underwear. I rolled up lots of toilet paper and put it in my underwear. I didn't know how to use sanitary napkins. That night when my mother came into my room to kiss me goodnight, I remarked casually, "Oh, Mom, I got my period." "That's wonderful!" she replied. The next day my Mom showed me how to use sanitary napkins. Menstruation was a subject that she talked about freely.

I do not get my period at regular intervals. It's really annoying to not know when it is coming. I get awful cramps that make me feel weak and peevish. I don't feel like doing anything. I'm afraid I'm not a very good companion during my period, but at least my mother hasn't thrown a party for me, yet!

"I Just Exploded" • Valerie, Age 13

For me having my period was a mysterious and strange thing. I first learned about it at school from a woman who made it sound very technical. It also sounded like a bad thing. She gave each of us a booklet to read on our own. I was afraid to tell my mother about what I had learned at school. I thought it might make her treat me differently. I went home and read the book to myself in the bathroom. It used big words that sounded strange. I was very worried about uncontrolled bleeding. I kept all these feelings from my mother. I really don't know why I was hiding these feelings from my mother. I guess I was so scared of her reaction to this new subject, I didn't want her to hate me.

Finally, I had so many feelings and questions that one day I just exploded. The tears ran and everything just felt like it was caving in. My mother held me and told me it was all right. Later we talked about it. My mother answered all my questions. When I got my first period, it was not scary. I found out it was all right and there was nothing to be scared of.

"You Shouldn't Worry" • Dawn, Age 12

Yes, it started on March 9th. It was during my 6th grade year. I woke up and blood was in my underwear. I was eleven years old and so scared I started to cry. I didn't know who else had started, so I felt very different. I also felt very self-conscious. I felt like everyone could see and sense I had started. I personally think it is very scary.

At first I was so irregular that I never knew when it would happen. Now, it has evened out and I know almost exactly when it will happen. Having your period isn't that bad. I mean, you feel a little more mature than people who haven't started. The thing that was scary was thinking, "Oh, no, I am growing up too fast." That thought really scared me. Another thing was the thought, "Oh, no, I can now get pregnant."

My life has changed a lot. I now am kinda grouchy at times, and I am not my normal carefree self—always laughing at stupid jokes that my friends say. Most of my friends haven't started their periods, so I feel I don't fit in anymore. I also hate my mood swings. Before I started, my life was very immature. Now, I feel I have matured and some friends haven't.

I really don't remember exactly what my Mom said to me. Only one thing is clear, "Don't worry, I'm here." She said this to me when I first started. My Mom is the person who taught me about menstruation. Also, she bought me many books about it and things to help me understand growing up and boys.

Only a few of my friends have started. We don't really talk about it because it really is kinda uncomfortable to talk about it in front of people who haven't started. My advice for someone who hasn't started is, "you shouldn't worry."

"My Older Sister Made Me Feel Better" • Bonnie, Age 13

I was eleven when I first got my period. It was summer and my birthday was about a week away. I'd been working as a Junior Counselor at a camp. They were having a show on bugs. Some other J.C.'s (Junior Counselors) didn't want to see it, so we went to the craft room and told scary stories. Just before I went to join them, I realized that I had to go to the bathroom. I went into the closest bathroom and pulled down my pants. As I sat down, I realized that there was blood on my panties. The blood scared me. Almost instantly, I realized that I'd just gotten my period. I didn't have a pad, so I just put some toilet paper there. When I came back from the bathroom, I felt embarrassed and silly the rest of the day. When I got home, I put on some new panties and a pad. Then I went and told my older sister. The first thing she said was, "MY little sister's a woman, now." I guess hearing that made me feel a little better.

Now it doesn't bother me at all. Really it's nothing to worry about. My earliest memory is sort of funny. My sister and a friend were talking about "Flo." I was totally confused. I asked and asked them about it, but they wouldn't tell me what they meant. Finally, they said something about blood and I got the hint. I asked my sister if "Flo" was your period, and it was. I instantly felt like a fool.

"The Guys Found Out" • Sonia, Age 13

I got my period in November. My friends and I were walking around Old Town after we had finished watching a movie. I had gone to the bathroom and I looked down. I couldn't believe that I had gotten my period! Luckily, I had 25 cents with me, and there was a pad machine in the bathroom. When I got out, I told my two best friends. Two guys were with us, and they soon figured out what had happened.

After that, the guys that were with us found out about my friends, also, who had gotten their periods. The guys started to treat us differently, as though they had to be careful about what they said. They also never pushed us around anymore. They started to treat us like porcelain, like they had to be very gentle with us.

I feel a little older having my period. I feel that I have more responsibilities, like being careful of what I do and say, so the entire world (in my case, 7th grade) doesn't know I got it. I think that is what is different now since I got my period. Now my friends and I talk about more stuff. I feel older and more mature.

My earliest memory about menstruation is when my best friend came up to me two days after I had gotten mine and said, "You'll never believe what happened when I got out of bed and looked down! I got it!" I do not remember who really told me about menstruation. I basically picked it up from discussions on TV and with my friends, and in science class when I was in 6th grade. Somewhere I learned what to do when you get it, and never tell your guy friends when it happens to you.

I feel that menstruation is a key that unlocks a whole new world of growing up. It is filled with responsibilities and adventures. Some of my friends have menstruated, but a few haven't. Sometimes my friends and I do talk about menstruation, but it is only usually discussed when it's "that time of the month" for one of us.

"We Had a Girl Talk Over Lunch" • Christy, Age 14

I got my period when I was eleven. I knew what it was, because a few of my friends had theirs already. My Mom had gotten me pads and stuff, so I was pretty much set. I told my Mom that I got my period, and she was really open to talking about it. She told me to feel free to talk to her about anything I wanted to. She told my Dad, which embarrassed me a little. She said that he understood about periods, too. He's a guy and it's really, really tough to talk to a guy, even my Dad, about periods and stuff like that.

When I was ten, my Mom took me out to lunch and we had what she calls a "girl talk." She told me that her mother, my grandmother, had never told her anything about menstruation. So when she got her first period, she was scared and didn't know what it was. She hid it for three days and then finally told her mother. My Mom didn't want me to be afraid or alarmed by something which was perfectly normal.

My period pretty much comes and goes regularly. A few times I've had to borrow clean shorts from friends because mine had blood on them. Nothing awful came of it. The worst thing that ever happened to me was once, when I was in a ballet class and I looked at my tights in the mirror, I saw blood on the back of them. I ran out and refused to take the class. I came out of the locker room with my jeans on.

Did you notice that even though the girls needed to talk with their mothers, and are glad their mothers gave them information, they still felt shy and embarrassed. Many girls believe that secrecy is necessary. Think about how you want to address the issue of secrecy with your daughter. Are code names ("Flo") all right, or do you want her to call menstruation by name? How do you want to involve the men in the family? What advice do you give her about asking male teachers to be excused, or hygiene "accidents," or boys teasing her? This is the time to be organizing your thoughts and talking with family members and other mothers. The next step is to make sure you know the facts so you can answer your daughter's questions.

Things To Do

- Re-read the girls' stories and jot down what the girls said about how their mothers offered information and emotional support.

- Write down the settings in which mothers and daughters discussed menstruation.

- Write down how you feel about the secrecy that girls believe they must keep about menstruation. Is it helpful, or not?

- Talk with other mothers of young daughters about their intentions for talks about menstruation. Compare notes and plans.

Things To Think About

- When you think about your menarche, is there a story in this section which is similar to yours?

- What role has your mother played in your knowledge and experience about menstruation? How do you want your role to be with your daughter?

- What do the girls in these stories still need to know about menstruation?

- What are the obstacles which girls face when having their periods at school?

- How might schools change to make it more convenient for girls?

Section II

Brush up on Basic Facts

College students tell me they don't know the basic facts about menstruation, aren't sure of their own anatomy, and don't know the vocabulary. They are reluctant to ask questions about their bodies, because they do not want to appear uninformed. Yet, some of them have wanted this information for years.

Young girls also want to know about their bodies, but may be afraid to ask. Before we can teach them, we must know the facts and feel comfortable talking about them. We also need to know about mood swings and hormones as well as about puberty and ovulation, pads and tampons.

Throughout this section there are words in *italics*. These words are also in the Glossary with expanded definitions written specifically for young girls.

Chapter 5

It's time to tell your daughter how her body is changing

Adolescence is the transition stage between childhood and adulthood. It is generally accepted that adolescence is from approximately 11 to 18 years of age. *Puberty* is reached during the first few years of adolescence. When a girl has reached puberty, it means that her body has sexually matured and she can reproduce. The definition of puberty is the same for boys.

The process of sexually maturing begins for a girl around eight years old, when the pituitary gland in her brain signals for an increased production of growth stimulating *hormones*. These hormones are secreted during the night while she sleeps. They stimulate body growth and also stimulate other sex related hormones to be released into her blood. When you start to think that your daughter must be growing out of her jeans and shoes while she sleeps, she has no doubt begun adolescence.

It is difficult to determine exactly when sexual maturation begins, because the effects of hormonal secretions are not immediately observable. Therefore, the beginning of sexual maturation is estimated by the observable secondary sex characteristics: height and weight increases, *breast development*, and *pubic hair* growth. The average age for the visible signs of sexual maturation is approximately 11 to 13 for girls. The normal onset can vary approximately two years in either direction and be considered within the normal range. For example, a girl could begin developing as early as 9 or as late as 15 years old and still be considered within the average range. It is not, however, difficult to determine when puberty is reached for girls. Once a girl has her first *menstrual cycle*, called *menarche* (MEN-arc-kee), then it is assumed that *sexual maturity* has been reached. Even though girls may not be able to become pregnant during their first *period*, they soon will be able to reproduce.

If you notice that your daughter is maturing earlier than 7 to 8 years of age, or if she is maturing earlier than any of the girls in her class or her friends, I recommend that you consult a pediatrician or family physician. Rarely are there problems with early maturation, but a visit to your physician can reduce doubts.

Predictors of Menarche

Mothers (and daughters) want to know how to predict the onset of that first *menstrual flow*, so they will be ready. There is no certainty in predicting menarche, but here are some predictors used by physicians. If any of these physical changes has already begun in your daughter, you should begin talking to her about *menstruation* now.

Typical sequence of development and events which predict menarche

- Breasts begin to develop with a slight elevation, called "the bud" stage. Next, nipples begin to pigment and the *areola* (ah-REE-o-la) surrounding each nipple increases in size. Some girls complain of pain or a lump on one side more than the other. This is normal. Reassure your daughter that she does not have a tumor or a problem. Many girls feel some breast tenderness or swollen breasts right before menarche.

- Pubic hair appears. In the early stage, one has to look closely to see the soft, light, down-like pubic hairs. During the next stage, the pubic hairs increase in number, become curlier, thicker, and usually darker. When the darker, thicker pubic hairs cover more of the outer *genitals* (the *mons* and the *labia majora*), this means menarche is rapidly approaching.

- *Axillary* (armpit) hair begins to grow after the breasts develop and pubic hair gets thicker. For some girls, axillary hair growth begins around the same time as breasts and pubic hair appear.

- The *uterus* and *vagina* have been growing since the beginning of puberty, but now the *labia majora* and *minora* and the *clitoris* increase in size. Also, vaginal mucous membranes become darker, more moist, and start producing a clear *mucous* discharge. Your daughter may ask you about the discharge and wonder if she has begun to menstruate. You can tell her that she has not yet begun her period, but this is a normal discharge and her body is getting ready to begin menstruation.

- Second permanent molars erupt, which are sometimes called "twelve-year-old" molars. They come in behind the first permanent molars and are the back teeth. These usually erupt after primary (also called "baby") cuspids and molars have been lost. Second permanent molars are usually the last teeth to erupt except for wisdom teeth.

- Growth in both height and weight begins and is called a *growth spurt*. For some girls, the growth spurt begins about the same time that breasts develop. For other girls, the growth spurt starts right before menarche, and for still others the growth spurt begins after menarche. During the growth spurt, girls usually grow as much as two to four inches in one year. Normally, girls grow taller first, then about six months later they increase in weight. The amount of weight needed to begin menarche is believed to be genetically determined. In order to begin menstruation, a girl needs to have approximately one fourth of her total body weight in body fat. Many physicians use 100 pounds as a benchmark. Therefore, girls who are taller and heavier than their peers are more likely to begin their periods earlier. For girls to continue menstruation they must maintain a slightly higher weight than when they first menstruated. Girls who are lean, involved in strenuous athletics, or ill for a long time may start their periods later than other girls their own age. Within a few years of menarche, girls complete their growth spurt and reach their adult height and weight. Researchers have found that girls who begin their growth spurt early, stop growing early and girls who begin their growth spurt later end it later. Regardless of when your daughter begins adolescence, it takes approximately three to four years for the growth spurt and sexual maturity to be achieved. Most girls reach their adult height and weight by ages fourteen to sixteen.

Medical professionals divide childhood and adolescent growth into five stages which they use to evaluate adolescent maturation. There is a Sexual Maturity Rating Scale for both Breast Development and Pubic Hair Growth. These rating scales are also known as Tanner Staging. There are diagrams and descriptions of these in the Glossary at the back of the book.

If you have questions regarding the timing of or any other concern about menarche, it is best to call a pediatrician, family physician, or family health clinic. There are rare cases when a girl might begin menarche too early or too late because of hormonal imbalance.

How Do I Explain It?

It is a real challenge to explain body changes to 7 or 8-year-old girls. Girls at this age cannot absorb the complicated details about menstruation in one lesson or discussion. Their physical clocks have sped ahead of their cognitive and emotional clocks. Therefore it is hard for them to immediately comprehend and visualize that internal changes are occurring inside their bodies which will lead to their maturation. In addition, they need time to feel comfortable enough with this subject in order to formulate their questions.

Beginning your first talk can be awkward for lots of reasons. Often mothers are a little nervous, daughters are busy doing something else, and menstruation seems far in the future. Most mothers report that they are able to get their courage and their daughters' attention by finding a quiet place. Mothers have told me about conversations in kitchens, bathrooms, living rooms, cars, cabins, restaurants. In fact, just about any relatively peaceful location where mother and daughter can be alone is good.

Talks about changing bodies and menstrual flow usually cause embarrassment for young girls. When asked, they are not sure why they feel embarrassed, but they do. I suspect that their embarrassment has to do with anything pertaining to the genital area, their lack of control of bodily processes and their fear of the unknown. These concerns can cause young girls to be fidgety, worried, or bashful, or to act disinterested. Even though your daughter may look or act uneasy, continue to have short talks with her because, whether or not it is apparent, she is listening to you.

I prepared the following short overview of maturation and the menstrual process written in language appropriate for young girls. There are diagrams on pages 55 and 56-57. There is a more in-depth explanation of menstruation and hormonal influences in the Advanced Explanation of Menstruation at the end of the book.

Girls' bodies begin to grow and mature when they are about 9 or 10 years old. All girls' bodies change and grow in order to become adult women. One day soon your body will begin to change. (Or your body has already begun to change.) The first change which you might see is that you grow a little taller and gain some weight. This is called the Growth Spurt. It is the beginning of growing hips, thighs and forming a waist for a mature woman's body. Other girls begin to grow breasts first. Either way, growth spurt or breast development is followed by soft, light, hair growing on your pubic area, called pubic hair. (You may want to comment on what a strange sounding word this is. In fact, many of these words are rather weird sounding to young ears.)

As a girl's body begins to mature, her sweat glands make more sweat or *perspiration*. During adolescence the perspiration begins to have a different stronger odor. We call this *body odor*. When you notice this, or if I do, we'll discuss using deodorant.

Another event that happens while girls' bodies are growing is called menstruation. It occurs for lots of girls between the ages of 11 to 13, but can be a little earlier or later for some girls. We will have to wait and see when you begin to mature and then begin to menstruate. (If your daughter is already showing outward signs of maturation, let her know that her body has begun already to mature and tell her about the signs which you have observed.)

After you say something similar to the above explanation, you can talk about "When I was your age..." Daughters enjoy hearing about their parents' history of growing up. It helps them to feel normal. This is particularly true with maturing and menstruating. It is always a good idea to add personal experiences about your growth spurt, pubic hair growth, and developing breasts.

After you talk about the early physical maturation, the next step is to discuss menstruation. In fact, many girls will ask about menstruation as soon as you finish talking about maturation and the growth spurt. Other girls may want to wait until a later time to begin thinking about menstruation; either way, you want to be prepared. Following is a menstruation overview.

Menstruation is a body function which occurs as girls grow and mature. Boys do not menstruate, so it is special and unique to girls. Girls' bodies begin to get ready to menstruate when special hormones are released from a small gland (pituitary gland) in the brain. These hormones are released when a girl is about 8 years old. These hormones travel through the blood vessels to organs in the *pelvis*.

Hormones act as messengers and signal a girl's body to begin to grow and develop—first on the inside and then a little later on the outside. Body parts that are unique to girls begin to grow, such as the uterus, vagina, and *ovaries*. After these have grown for a few years, the girl's body is ready to begin to menstruate.

Menstruation is what happens inside a woman's body that allows her to eventually have a baby. First an *ovum* (egg) matures. These eggs are very, very small and can only be seen with a microscope. Thousands of *ova* (eggs) are stored in little sacks called *follicles*. The follicles are located in the two ovaries. One ovary is located on the right and the other one is on the left side of the pelvic area.

Female Internal Sex Organs

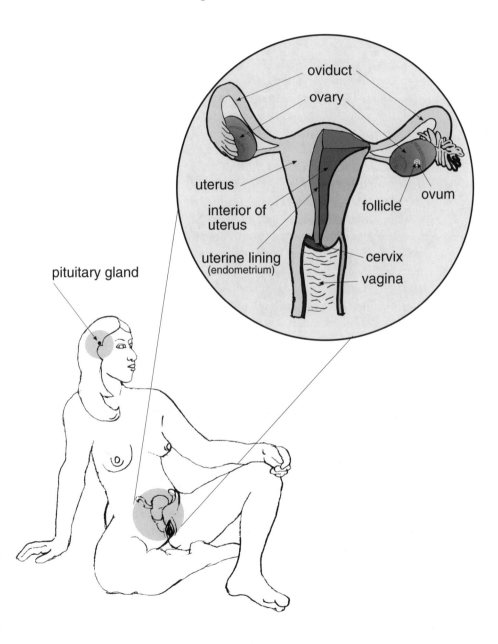

Menstrual Cycle by Days

Menstruation					Preovulation							
1	2	3	4	5	6	7	8	9	10	11	12	13
Uterine lining breaks down and is shed. Bleeding lasts 3-7 days.					Uterine lining builds up and ovum ripens.							

Just after menstruation starts, an ovum starts to mature. It takes about 14 to 17 days. An ovum, even when it is mature, is still very, very small and can be seen only with a microscope. When an ovum is ripe and ready, it jumps from its follicle inside an ovary into an *oviduct* (formerly called *Fallopian tube*). When an ovum jumps or is released from an ovary it is called *ovulation*. The ovum then travels down the oviduct until it reaches the top of the uterus. Some girls feel a slight twinge or pinch when they ovulate. Other girls do not feel anything. Either way is normal.

At the same time that an ovum is maturing in the ovary, the lining inside the uterus is building. *Uterine* lining is made of blood, cells, and mucus. Sometimes people refer to uterine lining as a *nest* where a fertilized ovum will grow during pregnancy. The uterine lining nourishes a developing ovum if it is *fertilized* by a *sperm*.

If an ovum is not fertilized, (which is the majority of the time,) then it, along with the build-up of blood, tissues, and *mucus* on the uterine lining, is washed out or *shed*. This shedding of uterine lining is called menstrual flow. Menstrual flow occurs about once a month. Menstrual flow is a natural, healthy loss of body tissues from the uterus. Menstrual flow is sometimes called menstrual blood, *bleeding,* or having a period.

The first few times a girl has menstrual flow, it may be so slight that a girl may not be certain that she has had her period and therefore, she might not know that she has started to menstruate. The menstrual flow is slight because the build-up of the uterine lining is thin in the beginning. When the menstrual flow comes down through the vagina, it usually looks more brown or dark red than a bright red. When girls are anticipating menstrual blood, they do not think that the brownish-red stain on their underpants is menstrual flow, but it could be. Some girls pay no attention to the brownish-red stain and go on as if nothing occurred. Sometimes girls think that they have injured

Ovulation		Premenstruation											
14	**15**	**16**	**17**	**18**	**19**	**20**	**21**	**22**	**23**	**24**	**25**	**26**	**27**	**28**
Ovum leaves ovary.		Ovum travels down the oviduct. Uterine lining continues to thicken.											

themselves. Please tell me if you have any stains. We can decide together whether we think that you have started to menstruate or not.

This is a lot of information. By the time you have looked at the diagrams, you and your daughter will be ready for a break. You can review this information as often as you need to. Anytime the opportunity presents itself, use it as an opening to repeat concepts, terms, and information. There is no such thing as too much repetition. High school teachers tell me that many 16-year-old students cannot correctly name their reproductive anatomy. Some do not know whether girls or boys have vaginas or scrotums.

Talks about menstruation usually involve discussions about sexual reproduction and fertilization of ovum. Many girls do not want to hear anything about this, while others will ask questions. Sexual reproduction is discussed in the Glossary. For now, let's continue with our explanation of menstruation, since girls and women menstruate regardless of whether they ever become pregnant

Right before menarche, some girls notice that their breasts become tender or swollen. Breast tenderness is one indicator that menstruation is on its way. It occurs because of the hormonal changes signaling menstruation, and usually lasts only a few days. Breast tenderness is often true for girls and women before their other menstrual periods as well.

Once the menstrual flow has begun, it normally lasts from three to five days. Three to six tablespoonfuls of menstrual blood are slowly discharged during these days and nights. Females differ in the number of days they flow, the amount, and the timing of flow. With experience, each girl figures out her own pattern.

Right after the menstrual flow has begun, the body begins to slowly build up the uterine lining while an ovum matures in an ovary. Once this process has started, it repeats itself each month into adulthood. This is why menstruation is thought of as a cycle, like the seasons of the year and the phases of the moon.

Each month, the female body repeats the menstrual cycle. During the first two to three years of menstruation, a girl's cycle can be irregular. This is very normal. The menstrual cycle is irregular both in terms of how many days a girl menstruates (or has menstrual flow) and how many days between periods. The reason is that young girls do not ovulate every month and, therefore, do not menstruate every month. Cycles become more regular as you get older.

Sometimes girls become iron-deficient which can lead to anemia. Approximately nine percent of girls aged twelve to fifteen and about eleven percent of girls aged sixteen to nineteen are iron-deficient. Their bodies need additional iron to build more red blood cells. Since the amount of red blood cells lost during menstruation depends on the heaviness of the flow, you will want to ask your daughter to tell you if she has heavy menstrual flow. You might say something like this:

If you menstruate more than three to five days, please let me know. Also, if your flow is heavy and you change your *pad* or *tampon* more frequently than every three to four hours, or if you use more pads each day than usual, please tell me. You might become low in iron either from loss of red blood cells during menstruation or a combination of menstruation and a diet low in iron. The only way to know for certain is to see your doctor. You might need to take multivitamins with iron.

The following two women, Christina and Colleen, recall different experiences learning about menstruation. Christina had no one to give her the basic information, while Colleen had a mother who was open and willing to talk about menstruation. Both girls felt relief when they learned the facts about menstruation. No matter how uncomfortable daughters act and feel during discussions about maturation or menstruation, having the basic information is always better than not having it.

Years of Experience

"Do Nuns Have Periods?" • Christina, Age 44

I had to leave my home when I was ten years old because my parents could not take care of my brother and me. My mother and I never talked about menstruation or growing up before I went to live in a foster home for a year and half. My foster mother, Mary, and I were close yet we did not have the occasion to talk about puberty or my body changing.

My first experience on becoming a woman was when I was eleven. The boys at school teased me about my hairy legs. I was so embarrassed. I went to my foster home one day and locked myself in the bathroom. Once I was in this safe place, I ran water for a bath and shaved my legs. I didn't even ask my foster Mom for permission. I was afraid that she would say, "No!" She did notice that I had shaved, but she didn't say a word to me. I just thought she didn't care if I shaved or not.

My brother and I did not get along. I asked to be placed into another foster home. My social worker placed me in a home for girls. It was also a Catholic school run by nuns. About 120 girls plus the staff lived there. The nuns never talked to us about our bodies and changes that were going on with us. One day, when I was in seventh grade and close to my twelfth birthday, I went to the bathroom before my next class. To my surprise, I had a small dot of blood on my underwear. I don't remember being scared. I didn't know what it meant either.

That summer I grew really fast. I grew five inches. My breasts started to develop. One of the girls at school said to me, "Don't you think it's about time for you to start wearing a bra?" I looked down. To my surprise, I had boobs! I had no idea what was happening to my body.

About six months passed before I spotted some blood again. By this time, some of my friends had also started to bleed. Somewhere along the line we figured out that we were starting to have our periods. No one ever explained what that term meant. We must have received this information from some older girls. Sister Elizabeth gave me a *sanitary belt* and some *sanitary pads*.

She explained how to use them without explaining what a period was. It never occurred to me to ask what was happening to my body. I guess Sister Elizabeth was too embarrassed to explain. I also wondered, "Do nuns have periods?"

When my daughter was nine, I had to tell her about menstruation and not be embarrassed like Sister Elizabeth. This is what I recall telling her:

"It is an honor to be a woman. When you start to have your period, you may experience stomach pains. These are known as cramps. You may feel sleepy or grouchy. This is normal. Your periods will often be irregular for the first year. We have periods so that we can have babies. Your womb (uterus) is where a baby can live for nine months while it develops and grows and gets ready for birth. A period is the body's way of getting ready for this miracle to happen.

Every month a lining of blood and tissues in the womb waits for an egg to be released from the ovary and the man's sperm to fertilize the egg. When the egg and sperm meet, they start to form a baby. If the egg does not get fertilized, the womb discharges this blood and lining down through the vagina and out through the vaginal opening which is between your legs. That's why you will need to wear a sanitary pad or tampon when you are having your menstrual flow. This whole process happens about once a month. Time varies for different women. For most women it is about every 28 days."

My daughter asked questions about what I told her. She was fairly well prepared for her first period. One embarrassing moment did come later. My daughter asked me to show her how to use a tampon. The physical act of showing her made me feel uneasy. I felt like I was all thumbs. She came home with a friend soon after the tampon lesson and asked me to show her friend how to use one. I guessed I had done a good job since she brought along another student. However, I drew the line and told my daughter that she would have to be the teacher for her friend. As I listened to her give directions to her friends, I thought about those nuns and wondered who had told them about menstruation.

"Moms Are a Big Help" • Colleen, Age 18

The first time I started my period, I was about thirteen years old. I had the stomach flu and was feeling pretty lousy. I didn't really know that I had started my period until I went to the bathroom.

While there, I noticed some spots of blood on my panties. I was pretty excited about the whole menstruation thing. In a matter of just a few minutes, I had been transformed from a young girl to a woman. It was really an exciting experience for me at that time.

I went to talk to my mother. At first she was worried. She had thought that something was seriously wrong since I had been sick. When I told her what happened, she was happy and relieved. My mom had been pretty honest and open about menstruation when I had asked her questions. She told me about when she was a teenager, and how she had to wear those cloth pads with the belts to hold them in place. Yuck! She always tried to make me feel better by telling me about the many different types of pads and tampons that were available. She reminded me that today each woman can choose the kind of pads or tampons that make her comfortable during her period.

Being able to talk to my mom about my period really helped me get through a somewhat confusing time. Knowing that my mom had gone through the same thing as I was going through made me feel a lot more comfortable with my newfound menstruation friend and also myself. I thought that if the same thing was happening to my mom, then I must be normal and have nothing to worry about. At the age of thirteen, I seemed to worry about almost everything. In those days it seemed that if you were at all different, you were doomed to be an outcast, forever.

After I told my mom about my blood spots, she gave me a pad to wear. I hated it! I felt as if I were a baby again wearing one of those big bulky diapers that won't let anything leak out. It was the worst feeling ever. Soon she took me to the local grocery store to shop for pads. It was definitely an interesting experience. I had never imagined that there were so many different types of protection to choose from. It was mind boggling. Today, I regard this shopping trip as one of the great "firsts" in my life. I remember leaning over the grocery cart in agony. I felt as if I'd gained 30 pounds in one day, and my whole body just seemed to scream in pain—a combination of period and flu.

When we got home, my mom gave me the "Birds and Bees" talk. I'm sure most mothers give some talk about sex around menstruation time. She told me that now I was approaching adulthood and could have children. Then she quickly added, "Wait a few years, PLEASE!" At that time, I had no interest in boys whatsoever, and the thought of sex repulsed me. Mom emphasized that I could still play sports because menstruation would not interfere with anything. As a matter of fact, it is quite healthy to exercise during menstruation time.

In addition to what my mom told me, I have learned through experience that I become a little moody because the hormones change as my body is flushing out the unneeded material. The hormones are changing so fast that they get a little out of balance. This causes me to become upset and easily agitated.

Luckily, I'm one of those women who is rarely affected by cramps. When I do get cramps, the best thing for me is to take a nap. This seems to stop the pain in about thirty minutes.

Although I felt like an instant woman the day I started my period, it has taken several years and many other experiences for me to really be a woman. I'm happy that I had my mom to help me that first day of my period and to guide me in later experiences of womanhood.

You now have a good review of menstrual terminology, examples of language appropriate for use with young girls, and easy to understand diagrams. Plus you have the two stories: Christina who was not prepared and Colleen who was prepared for menstruation. Which way do you want your daughter to remember her menarche?

Things To Do

Time to begin talks with your daughter.

- Find a quiet spot where you and your daughter can be alone.

- Begin a very simple discussion about her growing up and maturing.

- A few days later, or the following week, begin to talk with her about menstruation and show her the diagrams in this chapter.

- Keep the dialogue going, especially when opportunities present themselves, such as when an ad for sanitary pads comes on TV, or when someone else in your household has her period.

Things To Think About

- Was your early experience of menstruation like either Colleen's or Christina's?

- What were some feelings that the women in these stories had about their preparedness prior to beginning menstruation? How complete was their information?

- What would you like your daughter to remember about your talks together?

Chapter 6

What your daughter should know about pads and tampons

Girls want to know how to manage menstruation but are often afraid to ask. They worry about starting their periods and not being prepared. They worry about getting menstrual blood on their clothes, and how embarrassing that would be. They worry about what to do with used pads and tampons. Therefore, it is important that mothers start dialogues about pads and tampons as soon as talks about menstruation begin. More than likely your daughter has heard or will soon hear other girls talking about their hygiene horror stories. You probably remember talking with your girlfriends about someone getting her period when she was wearing white pants, how important it was to never let boys know you have your period, and how embarrassing it can be for girls to start their period unexpectedly. You have had years of experience learning to cope with the hygiene inconveniences and surprises associated with menstruation. No one learns how to manage these new responsibilities in one easy lesson, and your daughter will initially need your help in these matters.

Mothers who are relaxed about discussing the hygiene aspects of menstruation will help their daughters gain the confidence necessary to comfortably integrate these new routines into their daily lives. It helps to remember how you felt about hygiene mishaps—upset or embarrassed for a few days, but not damaged for life. Laughter really is the best approach; it can help everyone survive those traumatic months when menstruation is unpredictable and hygiene is unfamiliar.

Explaining Sanitary Pad and Tampon Use

When you explain sanitary pad and tampon use, try and remember stories or events that happened to you or your friends as you learned to wear pads or tampons. Daughters usually like this type of information. It helps connect them with you and your experiences of growing up. Using pads and tampons correctly is certainly an acquired ability. Many of the stories throughout this book recount humorous episodes with sanitary supplies. These accounts of learning to use pads and tampons will no doubt bring back memories.

Buy Pads Before She Starts

Today's choices of sanitary supplies are staggering compared to just a generation ago. It is a good idea to buy a variety of brands and sizes of pads and let your daughter experiment—before she gets her first period—in order to find the ones which feel most comfortable for her. Do not have her experiment with tampons before she gets her period. It is hard to get a tampon into and out of a dry vagina.

The two of you can go on a special shopping trip to buy the supplies, or you can ask her along on your weekly grocery trip. Young girls usually are embarrassed about buying sanitary products. If you do not accompany her on the buying trip, she probably will not go by herself. It takes time and dire necessity for most young girls to buy sanitary supplies on their own. Relating stories about your first trips to buy sanitary products can break the tension. Discussing the imagined horrors of classmates seeing them in the feminine hygiene aisle or check out counter, and what you each would do if this occurs, can provide laughs.

After the supplies are home, go over the specifics of each style with your daughter. Show her exactly how to use self-adhesive pads in her underpants. Explain to her that pads are made of absorbent material that catches menstrual flow. Maxi pads are for heavier flow days, and mini pads are for lighter flow days.

Girls normally like to have these talks with you in private. Many mothers report that after they discuss the use of pads, show the pads, and tell their daughters how they are worn, the girls are ready for a break. They are often initially "grossed out" or show a look of total disbelief. You can leave the supplies in the bathroom or your daughter's bedroom and simply suggest that she experiment. Later that day or the next, ask which pads she found most comfortable.

Even after menstruation has begun, it takes months for most girls to learn the particulars of their menstrual flow. Be sure to keep talking with your daughter about sanitary supplies after she begins her period. She may need more suggestions and guidance.

It is important to explain how often sanitary pads are to be changed. Physicians recommended that pads be changed every three to four hours. On heavy flow days, some girls change their pads every couple of hours. On lighter flow days, pads may be changed every four hours. In addition, you can explain to her which pads are good for overnight use.

When Is a Girl Ready for Tampons?

Your daughter will no doubt have heard about tampons, either how wonderful they are, or how disgusting they are, or both. Either way, she will have questions. In the past, it was believed that tampons were not good for girls to use before they were married or had babies. Today, physicians say tampons are medically safe for young girls. There is no medical reason for a girl not to use tampons. Your own belief, religion or culture, however, may influence your decision about your daughter using tampons.

Tampon use has caused some conflicts between mothers and daughters. One of the main concerns is the belief that tampons can break the hymen. Many people still believe that tampon use is inappropriate for virgins. Today, it is believed that young girls can break their hymens through a variety of everyday experiences, such as riding bicycles or horses, or playing sports. The hymen is a very delicate tissue which is easily torn. A girl can be a virgin even if the hymen is torn or doesn't bleed during sexual intercourse. If you have reservations about your daughter using tampons, you should discuss them with her.

Daughters need to understand the difference between tampons and pads. Tampons are different from sanitary pads because they absorb the menstrual flow before it leaves the vagina. For this reason, they must be inserted into the vagina. Tampons are small rolls of cotton or cotton-like substances with a string attached to one end. The string is used to pull the tampon out of the vagina. Some tampons come with plastic or cardboard applicators to help guide and insert the tampon up into the vagina. The advantage of using the applicator tampon is that it's easier to insert. Other tampons have no applicators and produce less waste because no cardboard or plastic is used. Since young people are ecologically-minded, the fact that tampons without applicators are the best ecological choice is something to remember to mention.

Many girls worry that tampons will get lost inside their bodies, but in fact this cannot happen. Tampons stay in the vagina and cannot travel anywhere else in the body. They cannot pass through the *cervix* into the uterus, because the cervix is too narrow. Most daughters need extra help learning how to use tampons. The instructions and diagrams on tampon boxes are usually confusing to young girls.

Girls usually like the idea of tampons, but may not be keen on touching themselves in the genital area. They need to know that they must use their fingers to open their labia majora and labia minora to guide the tampon into their vagina, even if they're using tampons with an applicator. Also, body position can help. Lying on her back, standing with one leg up on the edge of the bathtub, or sitting on the toilet can make it easier to slide the tampon into the vagina. When she is learning to use tampons she may want to wait for a heavier flow day. Getting a tampon in and out is easier on heavy flow days, but it may also be messier. This simple information can save your daughter a great deal of distress.

Removal of tampons simply involves pulling on the string so that the tampon slides out of the vaginal opening. It is important to remind your daughter to wash her hands after changing a tampon. When you say this, she may look at you with utter disgust. "How could you think that I would not know this?" she will likely ask.

On light menstrual days, it is usually more difficult to remove a tampon. The cotton substance will have expanded to catch the menstrual flow, and there may not be enough fluids to allow it to slide out smoothly. Instead of panicking, a girl can either raise one leg and place it on the toilet seat cover or bathtub, squat down, or lie on her back to cause the vaginal opening to expand. These are the same positions she may have used to insert the tampon. Also, remind her that she can ask for help from you or any experienced tampon user.

Changing Tampons

Physicians recommend that tampons be changed every three to four hours, the same as with pads. It is especially important to change tampons often to prevent a rare but serious illness called *Toxic Shock Syndrome* (TSS). It is believed that one cause of TSS is wearing the same tampon for a long period of time. The tampon may trap TSS bacterium in the vagina. TSS is caused by a bacterium infection which spreads quickly throughout the body and can lead to death. Symptoms include: high fever (usually over 102 degrees), diarrhea, vomiting, and a reddish rash like a sunburn. The rash is usually found on the stomach, back, and neck, but also can occur on hands and feet. After a while, the rash begins to peel. It is easiest to see peeling on palms of the hands and on the feet. If anyone has these signs they need to call a physician IMMEDIATELY. IF WEARING A TAMPON, REMOVE IT, AND BE SURE TO TELL THE PHYSICIAN THAT YOU HAD BEEN WEARING A TAMPON.

Girls' most frequent mistake with tampons is forgetting to remove them. Inform your daughter to check by inserting her index or middle finger deep inside her vagina to feel for a forgotten tampon. If she smells an unusual odor or has any other feeling that she has forgotten to remove a tampon, then it is always better to check. It is a must that your daughter be willing to check herself or go see a physician if she suspects that a tampon is lodged inside her vagina. Remind her about TSS. Since it is recommended to change a tampon every four hours, then it makes good sense to not go to sleep using a tampon. Instead use a pad while sleeping. The risk of TSS increases with the super absorbency tampons. Use as low an absorbency tampon as you can. There is more information about TSS in the Glossary. It is a rare, yet serious disease.

Disposal of Pads and Tampons

Your daughter will want to know how to dispose of used sanitary supplies. Pads should not be put in the toilet. They do not flush. The pads will clog the plumbing, the toilet will probably overflow, and out will come the used pads. Needless to say, this is embarrassing! It is certainly more embarrassing than throwing away the pad in the first place. Most toilets will allow a tampon to be flushed. Some of the tampon wrapper are flushable others are not. Read the box to determine if the wrappers can be flushed down the toilet. Daughters need to be reminded of this information, since it may be tempting to flush everything down the toilet. Instruct your daughter that most pads now come with an envelope-like wrapper to put used pads in before throwing them away. I suggest that you show your daughter how to do this with an unused pad so she'll know when the time comes. Also, if the pad doesn't have one of those wrappers, show your daughter how to wrap the used pads in toilet paper, and show her where to throw it away, especially in public places.

Alternatives to Standard Pads and Tampons

There are health professionals and ecologically concerned people who believe that using bleached or whitened pads and tampons contaminate the actual pads and tampons and the waste water from manufacturing them. In addition to the bleaching, pads and tampons are run through acid baths and caustic sodas during manufacturing which enhance absorbency, but which further expose females to contaminants. There are currently several styles and brands of unbleached pads and tampons available in health or natural food stores.

There is also a new feminine hygiene protection product called "Instead." Instead looks similar to a diaphragm and slides into the vagina right under the cervix. Instead catches the menstrual flow before it leaves the vagina and when removed it is disposable like a sanitary napkin.

Explaining "OTR"

The saying *"on the rag"* is an old expression. Girls are usually grossed out by the explanation, but I think they need to understand how their ancestors handled menstrual flow. There were no sanitary pads or napkins to buy—everything was made at home using clean cotton rags until approximately eighty years ago. Many of your grandmothers and great-grandmothers had to use rags to catch their menstrual flow. Remember Laura of *Little House on the Prairie* or *Anne of Green Gables*? Even though menstruation was not discussed, these girls would have had to use rags to catch their menstrual flow, then wash and reuse them. When women in those days said that they were "on the rag," they meant it.

It was not until 1921 when the first successful disposable hygiene napkins were manufactured by Kimberly-Clark. They were called Kotex. In 1927, Johnson & Johnson introduced Modess. These two companies had such a large share of the market for disposal hygiene napkins that most women referred to pads by either Kotex or Modess. Next came the first disposal tampon, Tampax, which was marketed in 1933. As you know, today there are many choices.

Today, the phrase "on the rag" has evolved to have negative connotations. Some males use the expression "on the rag" to mean that a woman is acting angrily or irrationally. For example, if a boy accuses a girl of being "on the rag," it usually has nothing to do with whether or not the girl has her period. It is not pleasant for a girl to be treated like this, and you can tell your daughter that if she is ever accused of being "on the rag," she can say, "That's so old," or some other neutral comeback, instead of acting insulted. Unfortunately, some males reveal their immaturity by using sexist language that is intended to intimidate girls and women.

Through the years, girls have devised code words and sayings to let each other know when it was their period. Some girls talk about their "red-headed friend" or their "cousin visiting from out of town." Hopefully, you can remember the code phrases for signaling your friends that it was "that time of the month." Your daughter will enjoy knowing these phrases and sayings.

Mastering the Fine Art of Using Pads and Tampons

"Stuck With Tampons" • Samantha, Age 24

I'm eleven years old. I'm sick. I'm home alone and I'm bored. I go into the bathroom and open my mom's "period drawer." The "period drawer" is my name for the place where my mom keeps all the good stuff; tampons that smell good and look like torpedoes, maxi pads that are like doll pillows, and mini pads that have glue on the back so you can glue them right onto your underwear.

My favorite things are the tampons. I get out the box with the lady in the flowing gown on the outside. I take out about ten tampons and open them up. I fill the sink with water, and I stick in the tampons, one by one. I love to watch them explode in the water—poof!—like a beautiful white flower. Even if you squeeze all the water out, they never open as beautifully as the first time.

I play with these tampons for about a half hour, and then I start getting bored again. I decide to stick a tampon inside me just like the pictures on the little piece of paper that came with the box. I find the place on the piece of paper, and I read the directions about 50 billion times. I unwrap my tampon. I put the applicator inside me, and I slowly, slowly push the tampon out of the applicator and into place inside my vagina. I did it! No problem. It doesn't hurt at all; this is great. I can't even feel it.

Now I think I'll take it out. Oh my, it's not coming out. It's stuck! My heart's beating really fast. I'll have to go to the doctor. I'll have to tell Dr. Gildersleeve that I was being stupid, and I stuck a tampon up me and now I can't get it out. He'll say, "You're right, you are stupid, now we'll have to operate." "No," I think. I'm not going to the doctor. I start to pull on the little string, and pull, and pull, until I feel like my whole body is going to go inside-out from all this pulling. Finally, it moves. As I keep pulling, it slowly comes out. Never, ever, will I stick another tampon inside myself, I vowed that day.

I'm thirteen-and-a-half years old. I'm really starting to wonder if I am normal. Maybe the nurses switched me with a boy in the hospital nursery. I have no period and small, I mean SMALL boobs. Two years ago, my friends and I spoke constantly about getting our periods. Now that THEY all have their periods, they instantly shut up. Amazing! Suddenly, they start throwing around phrases like: "girl trouble," "that time of the month," "my friend is visiting," "on the rag," and "my red-headed cousin from Brooklyn is here." Why can't they just say it, "We are all on our periods. We are mature, menstruating women, elevated to the status of martyrs five days out of every month, and you, Samantha, are a child." I can't believe these people are my friends.

I am fourteen years old. I am backpacking in the High Sierras with my best friend and her family. Guess who gets her period? That's right, me, Samantha, Queen for a Day! The best day of my entire life. Better than slow dancing with David. Better than my first kiss. I am woman, hear me roar! One small problem, no pads, only tampons, and not even real tampons at that. They are O.B. (stands for Obviously Bizarre) tampons. So we, (my best friend, her mom and I), all tramp into the forest, and I go behind the nearest tree. Sonja's mom is trying to explain to me where to put this O.B. thing. "Open the two lips of your vagina. Feel for the hole that's right after the hole you pee from." I am scared stiff thinking about my last experience with tampons. At the same time, I am so excited that my hands are shaking. I try and I try, but this little cotton wad wants to go everywhere but inside me. Exasperated, I come out from behind the tree. My underwear is around my ankles. "I can't find the hole."

We all give up. I fold a pair of dirty underwear and stick them in my underpants to wear as a maxi pad. My flow is close to zero, and we are going back down to civilization tomorrow. So I can make do with these panties. Every time I think nobody is looking, I stick my head between my legs to check for leaks. I am terrified my period is going to stop since it is so light. I just keep thinking, Blood! Blood! Blood!, hoping to send a message to my uterus to keep producing for a few days. The best thing is that I finally could feel as grown up as my friend, Sonja, who is actually a year younger than me.

When I get home, I tell my mom and later my older sister, Marie. The first thing Marie does is take me into the bathroom and tries to talk me into using a tampon. What is it with me and tampons? It's like a curse or something! So, she tries to show me how to put it in. I'm sitting on the toilet with my legs spread apart, and Marie is sort of looking at my vagina. She quickly jumps back and keeps giving me directions at the same time. This is as much attention as my sister has ever given to me in the whole entire time I have known her. I love this. When we come out of the bathroom, my mom asks, "Did you remember to take the applicator out?" She must think I am stupid or something. "No, Mom, I put the whole box in." I am completely embarrassed by her dumb questions.

I want to talk to someone, so I call up Best-Friend-Sonja. I tell her that my sister showed me how to use a tampon. Silence! Here we go again. Nobody wants to talk. So, I am in love with my period all by myself. I can change my maxi pad (which has a total of 1/8 teaspoon of blood on it), about 60 (well, not quite) times a day. One month passes and my wish for blood comes true. Does it ever come true! I bleed lots and lots for nine whole days. I can't believe it. Even I am getting sick of this period business.

I am seventeen years old. I am living with my aunt and uncle plus their four children. One of my cousins is eight years old. She wants to know everything about her body and mine. I let her come in the bathroom with me and watch how I put a tampon in. (I finally gave in. Now I even like tampons sometimes.) My cousin has also seen me use a maxi pad. I sometimes feel a bit uncomfortable, yet I'm really glad that I can let her see all the things that I was so desperately curious about. I certainly don't want her to do anything stupid like sticking a tampon in her vagina when she is not flowing, and her vagina is dry and then freak out when it gets stuck. After all, what are older cousins for?

"They Sell Supers in Washington" • Nadia, Age 23

I was in the ninth grade, fourteen years old, when I first got my period. The reason my age is so clear to me is that I felt behind the other girls. Everyone I knew, including my best friend, Cameron, and my sister, Dawn, who were both two years younger than me, already had their periods. I told my mother, "I got my period." Her reply was, "We'll get some pads. It should last about five days. If you're like me, the bleeding will be very light." That was it. I never asked anything more and nothing was offered to me. I guess I felt that was all there was to it.

After my first period, I didn't get it again for three months. These three months were the three months of summer vacation before starting my first year of high school. I have always been very physically active. Maybe this had something to do with my period never being regular. My period came when it wanted to, regardless of the calendar. I'd count the days and try to estimate when I would get it, so that I could be prepared.

I wanted to be especially careful if my period was supposed to come on a day when I would be going to school. The biggest laugh (if it happened to a friend), or the most embarrassing day (if it happened to you), would be the day you or another girl walked around school with a big red spot on the back of your pants, skirt or whatever it was you were wearing. This seemed to be a universal fear of us girls. We would do things like walk ahead of our friends so they could see if there was any sign of a red spot. We also told each other if we could see their pad.

Well, I never walked around with a red spot on my behind, but I can remember many times unexpectedly getting my period at school. I was never prepared. With me, this meant going to the school nurse. What an experience! The nurse gives you this pad, not just any pad. This pad would fit an elephant. You also got two safety pins so you could pin this pad to your underwear. With this elephant pad between your legs, you walk like you just got off of a horse. You have a bulge in the front of you and a bulge in the back of you because the pad is so long. To avoid this elephant pad, I would call my mother, and she would bring me a more modern pad, the small ones with the sticky stuff on the back so they stick to your underwear, no pins. Sometimes my mother would give permission, and I would go home from school. I have always wondered why the schools never supplied us with modern pads.

As I got a little older, I came to the conclusion that pads were a big inconvenience since I was very active and loved to swim. I spoke to my best friend, Carrie, about the fact that I wanted to try using tampons. She seemed to think this was a great idea. She thought we should try them together. It just so happened that we took a trip to Washington to stay on Carrie's grandma's ranch. We thought this would be the perfect time to go to the store to buy tampons. We were sure no one would recognize us in Washington. We set aside a day to walk to the nearest store. It was a small general store a few miles away. When we got there, we wandered around the store finally coming to rest on the aisle where the tampons were kept. We hoped no one would notice us there. Neither of us wanted to be the one to pick up the box of tampons. I'm not sure which one of us did, but we grabbed a box in a hurry. We ran to the cashier, paid for them, and ran out of the store. When we got outside of the store, we were both out of breath from being so nervous. We smiled at each other as if to say, "We made it!"

We started our walk back to the ranch. Of course, we wanted to look at what we had just bought. I took the box of tampons out of the bag. On the box, I noticed the big word, "Super." Somehow, I knew this meant size. I opened the box and took one out. It looked more like super-duper to me. I was angry, or should I say disappointed, that we were not more careful. Then I thought that maybe we could still use them. After all, we were just trying them out. When I mentioned this to Carrie, she said, "No way." Upset that we had not succeeded at what we had set out to do, I threw the open box of tampons on the ground. We continued our slow walk back to the ranch.

It rained the next day. We had to drive into town with Carrie's grandma. We knew we'd have to take the road where we abandoned the tampons. We also knew that the tampons would be all swollen with rain water. We worked hard to keep ourselves calm as we drove past. Today, it is still a joke between us. When Carrie and I see each other, all I have to do is mention "super," and we laugh and talk about our experience in Washington.

When we arrived home from Washington, both of us had our periods, so we walked to the store to try it one more time. This time having a better idea of what we wanted, or should I say a better idea of what we did not want. We were still nervous. This time we managed to buy the right size. We brought them back to Carrie's house. We opened the box and read all of the enclosed literature on tampons and how to use them. We also read about toxic shock syndrome. This frightened us, yet the thought of using pads the rest of our lives was frightening, also. We decided it was a risk worth taking. I took one tampon and the instructions into the bathroom where I tried it out. It wasn't that difficult. Sometimes it didn't feel just right, and I'd have to take it out and insert it again. Through much practice, I became a master at using tampons. Carrie did, too.

As you can tell, my mother and I didn't talk much about getting periods. I knew I would get it, but I didn't know why or what kind of changes were taking place in my body. I have grown up to feel uneducated about my own body. I still use books to educate myself about my body. I continue to talk to friends, like Carrie, about what my body is doing. She tells me about her changes, also.

Probably now you can remember your own escapades with feminine hygiene supplies. You are ready to answer any questions from your daughter. You are also able to anticipate many of her fears and address her concerns even if she does not ask.

Things To Do

- Take your daughter to the feminine hygiene aisle of the drug store or grocery store so that you can buy some pads and tampons. This will enable her to see the variety of sanitary supplies available. Your shopping trip together also gives your daughter the experience of being seen in this particular aisle without dying of embarrassment, which many girls swear they will do.

- Have the menstruating women in the household put their sanitary supplies in a basket or box on the back of the toilet. This practice makes supplies convenient for the women to use, and also sparks questions by family members who may want to talk more about menstruation, including the boys and men in the house. By placing sanitary supplies out in the open, the shame and secretiveness that are unnecessarily associated with menstruation are reduced.

- Measure three to eight tablespoons of water and put red food coloring in it. This is the average amount of menstrual flow that women discharge each month. Take a pad or tampon and let your daughter experiment with absorbing this amount of liquid.

Things To Think About

- Do you recall any humorous episodes involving menstruation that made you feel closer to a girlfriend or family member? Have you shared your remembrances with her lately, or ever? Have you told your daughter about these experiences?

- What did your mother or another significant female in your life teach you about using tampons? Are you prepared to teach your daughter about tampon use?

- Why have you chosen the feminine hygiene products you now use?

- What friends do you talk to about menstruation? What family members do you feel comfortable talking to about menstruation?

Chapter 7

Mood swings, cramps, and PMS are a lot to cope with

Any parent of an adolescent can tell you that mood swings are normal. One moment your daughter or son is cheerful and loving, and the next moment she or he storms out screaming that you don't understand anything. In addition to the normal emotional changes associated with adolescence, many young girls must also cope with *Premenstrual Syndrome* and *cramps*. These new realities in a young girl's life can cause great stress in her family environment. Unfortunately, our culture adds fuel to the emotional fire with its unrealistic weight and beauty expectations for maturing females.

There is very little scientific research to shed light on why such mood swings occur, only that they do. Some researchers think the unpredictable emotional upheaval in girls is caused by hormonal changes, and some think that societal pressure on teens is the culprit. Probably both contribute. It is important to talk to your daughter about her mood swings. It will make her feel better to know they are normal.

Raging Hormones

Many medical researchers believe that since several female hormones begin production during puberty, these hormones play a part in emotional ups and downs. However, there are no clinical or blood tests to confirm this relationship. Many boys in this age group also go through similar mood swings. Their temperamental changes, however, are not usually attributed to their increased hormone production. More research is clearly needed to determine what part hormones play in adolescent moodiness.

A group of researchers did study both women and men's mood fluctuations during a thirty-day-month. They found that both have mood fluctuations during the month, even though men do not have the wide variation in hormonal levels that women have. So mood swings should not be blamed entirely on hormones.

The following graph of female hormone production during a typical 28 day cycle is powerful evidence that significant chemical changes take place within the bodies of menstruating girls. Whether these are the cause for mood swings is yet to be determined.

Female Hormones

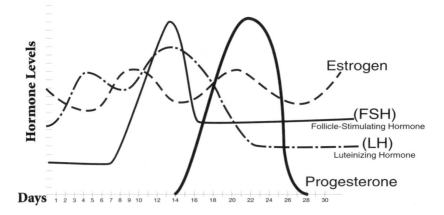

Premenarche (before the first period) mood swings have also not been studied very widely. It does, however, appear that once hormones are secreted during early adolescence (around 8 or 9 years old), many girls start to experience mood swings. Since most people are unaware that these hormones are in the bloodstream of such young girls, it is easy to understand how young girls' moods can be misinterpreted.

Most girls are as upset by their unpredictable moodiness as are the adults around them. Often they're not aware of what has caused their outbursts of tears, anger, or even rage. They may cry even when they try hard not to. They don't intend to say mean-spirited things to those they love, but the words come out anyway.

At the first signs of unexplained mood swings, (which could be from 8 to 11 years of age), begin to keep track of your daughter's "out of the blue" moodiness on a calendar. There may be a cycle or pattern to her temperamental behavior. Keep track for at least three to six months before deciding if there is a pattern. Some mothers report that their daughters' feelings appear to be more easily hurt around the same time each month. For example, daughters may be more moody or have less resiliency to criticism around the first of most months, but may handle the same criticism better during the middle to end of the month. If you know that some times of the month are more difficult for your daughter, wait a few days to give her a suggestion, and she may more readily receive it or at least not reject it outright.

Cultural Pressures

Some researchers think female adolescent mood swings, both pre and postmenarcheal, are caused by additional pressure from parents, teachers, friends, and the media rather than hormonal fluctuations. The three basic pressures are: looking and acting perfect, being liked, and doing well in school. Unfortunately, by early adolescence, girls have learned that it is sometimes best not to show that they know more than boys (or other girls for that matter.) So one basic pressure (to achieve) is in direct conflict with another (to be liked). Talk about a double bind! Since most adolescent girls cannot live up to all these goals, frustrations build and they let them out through tears, screams, pouts, or rage.

Young girls live in a world that gives them conflicting messages. Television shows, films, music videos, and advertisements encourage them to be thin, beautiful sex objects at the same time that parents and teachers encourage them to be intelligent, motivated, healthy, and happy students. Your daughter is growing and maturing, and a certain amount of weight gain is normal and necessary during adolescence. Make certain to explain to her that her body growth is normal and that this is the time to eat a healthy, balanced diet. Together you can plan out a daily food guide. If you would like help, your pediatrician or clinic, can provide materials on teenage nutritional requirements.

Becoming aware of one's changing body is all part of growing up and maturing. Young adolescent girls, however, think that their nose, feet, or hair is all wrong, too big, too small, or too something. You name it, and a girl can feel dissatisfied with something about herself at this stage. Our society ceaselessly tries to convince us that we're not okay as we are, that we need certain products and services in order to be acceptable. We would not be in the market for things to make us more attractive if we didn't buy in to this way of thinking. Unfortunately, comparing bodies is part of evaluating how we fit into the world. Adolescent girls are especially vulnerable to criticism, teasing and harassment about their bodies and, for this reason, they need adult acceptance and guidance.

The message is clear for the adults. We must encourage our daughters to accept their bodies as they begin the journey to womanhood. However, no one can live up to the unachievable media messages. Even the models who we admire complain that they are not quite "right" yet, they want to buff up here, slim down there. Mothers and fathers are the primary defense to counteract these dangerous messages which cause negative self-images in daughters. The focus must be on what is inside us which makes each of us special, not on our bodies.

Learning to accept our body is difficult for most females at any time of life. With this in mind, respect your daughter's feelings and protect her from potentially embarrassing situations whenever possible. Help her learn social rules, respect her need for privacy, take her concerns seriously, and most of all do not make fun of her. She is acting in earnest as she struggles with her changing body and her evolving self awareness as an adolescent.

Adolescent girls also feel pressure to be more independent of their parents, yet often they do not feel safe at school or in their communities. Young girls, when asked, talk about their fear of being physically attacked or verbally ridiculed. This type of fear or apprehension certainly can cause great frustration for girls who are trying to achieve some sense of control in their lives. It helps for parents to discuss independence and safety with their daughters. Find out what your daughter worries about, and what she really wants. If she is worried about being attacked, enroll her in a self-defense class. If school is not safe, meet with the principal and try and change things. Often friends push for privileges that your daughter may not feel ready for. Listen closely to what she says, but you make the decision. Then stick to it. Often your daughter will be grateful for the limits—as long as she knows that you will expand her privileges as she gets older.

What To Do About the Outbursts

I've talked about ways to avoid the emotional outbursts: don't bring up difficult subjects when she's moody, stay aware of her cycle and adjust your demands, support her accomplishments and talk about her fears. What do you do if she's yelling and screaming right now?

- Do not yell back. It doesn't do any good and just escalates the conflict.

- Tell her "I'm listening and I know you are upset. I don't have anything helpful to say to you right now. Let's talk later."

- If she continues to yell, tell her to go to her room.

- If she cries, hold her and comfort her (as long as she is quieting down.)

- Try and share responsibility. You can say something like, "We both need time to think about this. We'll talk more later."

- As she quiets down, show her you are not mad at her (just her behavior). Offer her a snack or include her in something you are doing.

One last thought on strong emotions. If your daughter threatens harm or violence against herself or others, is persistently in depressed moods, has falling or failing grades, begins to skip or drops out of school, shows little or no interest in her life in or out of school, then she needs help immediately. These are signs that something is seriously troubling her. These behaviors are not common to normal adolescent development. Get help; consult your family physician, pediatrician, or school counselor for a referral to a counselor who specializes in psychological therapy for adolescents.

The good news is that daughters do survive these years of tears, anger, rebellion, and change—and so do parents. This period (no pun intended) is a time of great struggle for your daughter, but she can come through it as a healthy, well-adjusted young woman, with the appropriate acceptance and patience from you and the others in your family.

Menstrual Cramps

You also need to discuss menstrual cramps with your daughter. Most young girls have not heard much about cramps, but as they grow older they are likely to hear about them from other girls. If you have not told your daughter about cramps, then she is most probably going to be worried or panicked when other girls describe menstrual cramps and pain.

Some females have cramps or pain and others do not. Females who have cramps tend to have them in their abdominal area or lower back. Current estimates are that 50 to 75 percent of female adolescents and young adults have some menstrual discomfort. Women have a wide range of normal body responses to menstruation, childbirth, and menopause. Some women have very little, if any, discomfort, while others have a great deal of pain. This lack of predictability is one reason why females have often been wrongly told that menstrual pain is "all in their head."

Just because mothers do not have cramps does not mean that their daughters will not have cramps. Likewise, neither is it true that because a mother has cramps her daughter will have them. In addition, girls' bodies change with age. Girls who don't experience cramping during their early years of menstruation, may begin to have them, and girls with cramping can seemingly outgrow them. Since the occurrence of cramping is very difficult to predict, it is important to let your daughter know that she can talk with you about her concerns, fears, aches and pains.

Cramps happen when muscles in the uterus contract to help push out or shed uterine lining. A hormone-like substance called prostaglandin (pross-tuh-GLAN-din) actually causes the cramps. Today, we know that females with increased levels of prostaglandins tend to report higher incidence of cramping during menstruation. Severe cramping can result in nausea and headaches. Since it is not known whether or not your daughter will have menstrual cramps, it is best to tell her that some females have cramps while others have none or very little pain during menstruation. Ask your daughter to tell you if she feels abdominal and lower back cramps or pain. Together you can decide what course of action to take. There are helpful over-the-counter medication for menstrual pain and headaches, such as Advil and Alleve. Seeing a physician is recommended if your daughter's pain persists even after these over-the-counter medications are taken.

If you or your daughter has menstrual cramps, here are a few suggestions which do not require medications. Physicians routinely recommend reducing salty foods, caffeinated drinks, chocolate, and sweets. By decreasing or eliminating these foods, you retain less water and cramps are relieved. Eat a healthy diet high in carbohydrates, such as fruits, vegetables, grains, cereals, and low in fats, such as butter, salad dressing, cooking oil, mayonnaise. Moderate physical aerobic exercise, for example, jogging, swimming, bicycling, etc. is also helpful in reducing cramps. Some girls and women use a warm heating pad or water bottle to relieve their cramps. Back and lower back massages also help to reduce pain and discomfort from cramps. Other women drink herbal teas to reduce their menstrual cramps. Raspberry leaf tea is the most commonly recommended. In addition, some women take calcium and magnesium supplements several days before their period begins and then continue until their flow ends. Other women find that vitamin B-6 or a general B-complex supplement during their period helps reduce pain. Consult your physician before giving your daughter supplements.

Menstrual pain is a leading cause of school absences for teenage girls. Check with your daughter's school and see if the school nurse (or someone else at the school) dispenses over-the-counter medications for menstrual cramps. Are girls sent home? Are parents notified? Can girls bring their own over-the-counter medications to school? Are girls allowed to leave class to take these medications or attend to other menstrual needs? Each school has its policies for accommodating young girls with their menstrual cycle. If you find that the school's policies are inflexible or unrealistic of young girls' needs for time, privacy, and supportive personnel, then there are two basic courses of action. First, you and your daughter can plan a strategy specific for her needs and concerns. Second, you can work to change school policies to meet the needs of young girls who require flexibility and support as they learn about their maturing bodies.

Explaining Premenstrual Syndrome

Menstrual cramps are not part of *Premenstrual Syndrome* (PMS). It is helpful to explain that menstrual cramps occur during menstrual flow, whereas, PMS occurs one to two weeks before the menstrual flow begins and goes away once the period has begun.

PMS is not very well understood. PMS occurs after ovulation when progesterone levels rise in relationship to *estrogen*. This is a natural process, but it is still unclear why some females have symptoms, while others do not. PMS symptoms include headaches, weight gain, breast tenderness due to water retention, acne outbreaks, increased cravings for foods high in sugar or salt, and feelings of irritability or depression. Anyone can have one, two, or more of these symptoms and not have PMS. PMS is more difficult to diagnose than most people think. Symptoms may be related to PMS *only* if they begin after ovulation and go away when the menstrual flow begins. If the symptoms persist after the period, they are not caused by the same hormonal relationship as PMS.

PMS is controversial both in medical literature and common experience. This syndrome is difficult for medical researchers to study, diagnose, and treat because symptoms present in some women may not be present in others. PMS appears to be reported by about 50% of menstruating females. To make it even more perplexing to study, women with symptoms of PMS say that some months are better or worse than others.

In many girls, PMS symptoms can be treated by following the suggestions for relieving cramps. It is most important to reduce caffeine intake. Next, encourage aerobic exercise. After following these suggestions, if your daughter continues to suffer from PMS, it is time to consult your health care provider.

Unfortunately, PMS has become the brunt of jokes and sexist comments. This makes it all the more important for mothers to pay attention to their daughter's complaints and concerns. By listening to daughters, mothers can help them get the information they need to become experts about their bodies.

The next stories call our attention to the importance of feeling accepted and being normal. You can help your daughter by reassuring her these changes are normal, and by helping her get medical advice when she needs it.

Feeling Accepted

"Anne Frank Was Normal" • Jacque, Age 26

I started menstruating in the fifth grade. I had just turned eleven. I started before most of my friends. I also developed physically before most of them. I felt isolated from many of my friends because things were happening to my body that did not seem to be happening to them. I believed that if I told them they would treat me like a freak. I am grateful that I had a rather small chest. I was going through body changes, but at least most of them did not show. It seemed to me that the chesty girls had a tougher time with the whole experience. They received more attention and more teasing. A girl in my class was severely chided and put down by an adult at the school for not wearing a bra. I felt sorry for her. She was a beautiful girl and the criticism only made her feel awkward and ugly.

Most of the attitudes of the adults in my personal life did not change towards me except for my dad. I always looked boyish when I was young. Even though I was changing, it did not show that much. I adored my dad. I watched football with him and helped him fix his car. When I hit puberty and began to menstruate, he withdrew from me. At first it hurt a great deal. Then I came to understand that he is not comfortable with women. If he was not comfortable with women, he must not be comfortable with me, a young woman. It was tough to come to terms with my dad's rejection. I missed his special attention that I got before puberty.

When I was going through the growth spurts and breast development, I always wished for someone to talk to; someone who could reassure me that I was "normal." My mother, like my father, has never been comfortable talking about menstruation. It has been one of those subjects that is never brought up in conversations. Instead of talking to someone about the changes occurring inside of me, I decided to keep it to myself. I then started to worry about it. Was I normal? Was I getting some dread disease? Did I have to go to the doctor? Having my period made me feel cramped and irritated. Was that normal? When I asked my mother why my breasts hurt she told me, "Don't worry about it. It will go away." I wish she could have explained more and been more helpful.

When I finally reached the sixth grade, we were assigned to read *The Diary of Anne Frank*. I remember reading about her feelings about menstruation and that she seemed to feel cramped and bloated, also. I thought maybe I am a normal adolescent, if someone else could have the same feelings that I have. Perhaps other girls have felt the same.

Today when I think about my experiences as an eleven-year-old, I wonder why I worried about my body so much. I remember some of the worries my friends went through such as: "If I kiss a boy, will I get pregnant?" I never had a problem with that one.

Throughout the time between eleven and eighteen, I was worried about being normal. Since that time, I gathered the courage to ask a gynecologist about being normal. She answered, "You are disgustingly healthy and perfectly normal." What a relief. Her answer has allowed me to become relaxed and be comfortable with myself and my normal menstruation.

"My Aunt, My Mom, and My Friends All Helped Me" • Jami, Age 35

I started my period the summer after I graduated from sixth grade. It was June, 1964, and I was eleven years old—soon to be twelve (in three months). Right after school let out for the summer, I went to stay at Nana Kishimoto's for a few weeks like I normally did each summer. It was mid-afternoon and I went to the bathroom to pee. When I wiped myself, there was blood on the toilet paper. I must say I was a bit startled to see blood on the paper. I knew about menstruation, yet I didn't think I would start my period quite this soon.

I'm sure glad my period started on a Saturday because Auntie Jane was home and not at work. If it had been just Nana Kishimoto and me in the house alone that day, my first menstruation wouldn't have gone so smoothly. Nana Kish didn't speak much English. Auntie Jane and I went to the store together. Auntie Jane wanted to buy me my very own belt and a box of pads. This way I would have my own personal menstruation supplies, and that would make it more official. As I look back on the event, I can see how tickled Auntie Jane was that she was able to share this experience with me. I was like a daughter to her since she never had any children of her own. I sometimes called her my second mother. I still do. Going through the experience of my first menstruation together bonded us even closer. My mom was kind of surprised that I had started so soon. She was reassuring that this was the most natural thing in the world to be happening to me. She also said this made me a young woman now.

During my first menstruation experience, I didn't have cramps or a heavy blood flow. But I was not very regular each month. As I grew older, cramps and heavy bleeding developed. Some months were so bad that I really thought I was going to bleed to death. My mom would have to calm me down and reassure me that I would not bleed to death from menstruation, and that I would survive this. You could have fooled me! But, she was right. In junior high school, it was not unusual for me to have to stay at home the first few days of my period. I would be doubled over in bed with a heating pad because my cramps were so bad. I would bleed so much that I would go through a pad in no time flat. This is when I started hating this period stuff each month. This was truly the "curse" that I had heard others call their period. I now knew what they meant by that term. Some women actually refer to their period as being their "little friend." I guess some women are relieved and happy when they get their period because it means that they are not pregnant.

When I was in the eighth grade, my best friend, Pat, introduced me to the wonderful world of tampons. I'll never forget that day. We were at her house the day she tried to get me to use one. We were going to a swim party that afternoon. I told Pat that I'd have to stay out of the water because I still had my period. She didn't think that should stop me. After all, there were such things as tampons, and you could swim if you used them.

I had never thought of using them. In those days people believed that nice girls shouldn't use tampons. Using them meant that the girl was probably fooling around with a boy and having sex. This thought ran through my mind. And I knew that my boyfriend thought the same as well. (He turned out to be my future husband.) I wanted to be a virgin when I got married. I didn't want the use of a tampon to a create doubt about my virginity.

Pat was, however, worldly in my eyes. She had traveled to many foreign countries. Her father was in the military, and she was known as an Army Brat. Pat insisted that tampons did not take away a girl's virginity. She sounded very convincing. I decided to trust Pat and let her walk me through this. She handed me a tampon and told me to go into the bathroom. She would coach me from the other side of the bathroom door. I was scared to death at the thought of putting that thing inside my vagina. Yet the more I thought about all the good things Pat told me about tampons, including never having to wear those nasty ole sanitary napkins again, the more I wanted to give it a try.

I did just as Pat instructed. It wouldn't go in. Pat told me to relax so that my vaginal muscles wouldn't constrict and make the hole too small for the tampon. I finally got it part way in. The rest just wouldn't go up any further. I started to panic thinking this stupid thing was going to be stuck in me forever.

Pat stayed with me. She kept talking me through this ordeal. She then told me to lift my butt off the floor a little so my vaginal passage way would be at a tilt. She thought maybe it would go in better that way. Well, it didn't. I was too tight and too dry. By this time I had had enough. I pulled the tampon out. I yelled to Pat, "I can't do this." I was sweating bullets at this point and decided to get dressed.

When I opened the bathroom door, there was Pat's face glaring at me with total disappointment and frustration. I pleaded with her that this was not for me. I said that I was not built to wear one of these things. She wouldn't hear of it. She handed me another tampon and told me to get back in there and stop being such a baby.

I thought to myself, "She's not going to let me out of this bathroom until I do this." I got down on the floor on my back, with my legs up, and just pushed the tampon in. At this point, I realized it really didn't hurt going in and this wasn't so bad. I'm really glad Pat had been so persistent with me about trying tampons that day. She knew that once I got the hang of it, I would love them and never go back to using pads again. She was right. I have been free from those bulky pads ever since.

Things got even better with regards to my periods. When I was a senior in high school, I got back together with my boyfriend, Mark. We had first met in the ninth grade. Then we went to different high schools. Mark's mother, Betsy, was a registered nurse. Betsy and I became very close. She knew how much I suffered with those lousy menstrual cramps each month. She helped me get a prescription for pain relievers. They were a mild pain killer that did not affect my ability to function normally. This meant that they didn't make me sleepy. Those pills were heaven sent. I can't tell you what a blessing it was to have those pills for the first few days of my period each month. I was really cooking now! I had my tampons and my pain killers. Who could ask for anything more? When that period rolled around each month, I hardly even noticed it. Life was good again.

The mood swings, hormonal changes, cramps, grouchiness, cultural, school, and family pressures are challenging for all girls and their parents. While adolescent girls grow into their new bodies with all their physical and emotional changes, it takes patience, understanding and acceptance by the family.

Things To Do

• Buy or make two calendars so that you and your daughter can each record a more accurate picture of mood swings, both premenarcheal and premenstrual, and the length and nature of each menstrual cycle. It is a fairly common occurrence for females who live together to begin to menstruate at about the same time. No one is certain why this happens, but it does and it is called Menstrual Synchrony. This synchronizing of menstrual cycles occurs with both related (mothers, daughters) and unrelated females (dorm roommates.)

- Plan one or two activities which you and your daughter like to do together. When one or the other of you is upset or frustrated, then either one of you can call time out and ask for the activity. The activity could be a walk around the block, watching 30 minutes of agreed upon television, playing catch or volleyball, going for a short bike ride. Our family's favorite is a long, loud, and rousing piano duet of "Heart and Soul." It is difficult to stay mad or frustrated after these activities. Be creative with ways to reduce stress between you and your daughter.

Things To Think About

- The women in these stories were concerned about being normal. Were their experiences normal? Do you feel your menstruation was normal as a young girl? Do you think that your daughter will feel her physical development and emotional swings are normal?

- Do you remember if you had mood swings before you began your menarche? Maybe you can ask your mother, father, or older sibling.

- What emotional symptoms have you experienced with menstruation, if any? What are your experiences with PMS? Why are there so many jokes about it?

- What authorities do you trust when it comes to menstrual problems? Think of all the people who might have information about menstruation whom you would be willing to ask if you or your daughter had a problem.

- Did you physically develop early or late for your age and friends? How did the timing of your maturation make you feel?

Section III

Face to Face

It is important that you start the short dialogues about maturation and menstruation early in your daughter's development so communication lines can be kept open. If your daughter is prepared for menstruation ahead of time, she will be informed and confident about her body as it changes. She also will have learned from you that it is acceptable to ask questions about her body. And when the big day comes, you want her to feel comfortable with her father and brothers, and feel it is something to celebrate.

Chapter 8

Sometimes it's hard to talk about things, but you can do it!

Just as you have used a variety of persuasive strategies to convince your daughter to do her homework, practice a musical instrument, or tell you why she is upset, you can also employ similar techniques to teach her about menstruation. Parents often imagine that the most important talks they'll have with their children will take place in a quiet setting at a particular time that they have carefully set aside. In fact, most of the important lessons we teach our kids are taught informally and when we least expect to address certain questions—for example, while we are rushing to get out of the house, driving to the market, or stepping out of the shower. You'll be in the middle of rush hour traffic, thinking about the endless errands that need to get done, and your child will suddenly ask you about God...sex...menstruation. The communication ideas in this chapter combined with the activities and information from the previous chapters will prepare you for this, as well as for the very typical situation in which you try to bring up the subject of menstruation, and your daughter tries to avoid it out of embarrassment or disinterest.

The Teaching Process

How many times have you reminded your daughter to brush her teeth? Told her about the importance of dental health? Talked to her about the proper way to use a toothbrush? Just as there is no such thing as only One Big Talk about this important subject, there is also no such thing as having only One Big Talk about menstruation. As with so many other lessons we teach our children, teaching your daughter about menstruation is an ongoing process.

The concepts and vocabulary which you will be introducing to your daughter are not all that easy to understand and remember— even for older girls or for women. At eight or nine years old, girls cannot be expected to learn everything they need to know about this complicated process in one easy lesson. It will be up to you to reintroduce the subject of menstruation a number of times, and in a number of different ways, throughout this stage in your daughter's life. Assuming that your daughter has "gotten it" after only one or two brief talks is wishful thinking. It is your persistence that means the difference between her feeling apprehensive or confident.

Another important thing to remember about communication is that it's not only what we say, but how we say it. Educational research informs us that much of what we learn at school is not what the instructor is formally teaching. Daughters are more likely to learn from what the teacher says as an aside, from her body language, or her emotional tone, than from a lecture or formal discussion.

One daughter casually mentioned to her mother, "Mrs. James is ashamed of menstruation."

"How do you know that?" her mother asked.

The daughter continued, "Every time she starts talking about it, she looks at the floor. She never looks us in the eye the way she does when she is teaching history."

Your daughter will learn your attitude toward menstruation in much the same way. She will watch what you do as you speak, and listen to how you state what you're telling her. In addition, she will observe her father's and other adults' reactions to the subject of menstruation. The non-verbal behavior and reactions of adults communicate attitude as well as information.

As already mentioned, you must prepare for menstruation to become a topic of discussion at odd times and in incongruous settings. Daughters often ask questions at inappropriate moments. (Have you noticed?) Therefore, mothers need to be ready to teach about menstruation quickly and on the fly. Fortunately, a daughter neither requires nor desires a long scientific explanation of the menstrual cycle when asking, "What if I have a stain on the back of my clothes? How will I know if I started my period, or just sat in something yucky?" This is a common fear and question for most young girls. A good response is simply to advise her to go to the rest room and check her underpants. If there is a brownish-to-red color of stain on the crotch, then she has probably started her period. If not, then she has more than likely sat in something yucky. You will want, however, to remember your daughter's questions and return to them later that day or the next day after you have thought more about them. These kinds of questions, "What do I do if...?" lend themselves to brainstorming for many possible solutions.

There are two places where teaching on the fly is likely to occur: in the car and in the kitchen. Since you are busy driving or cooking and are not focused on your daughter, she feels safe and in control. You must be spontaneous and rely on your own knowledge and experiences. This is certainly not the time for diagrams or other visual aids. At these teaching times, you will be glad that you wrote your own menstrual story, that you familiarized yourself with the other young girls's feelings and fears, and that you took the time to refresh your memory on physiology and adolescent emotions. You may get quite nervous talking on the fly if you believe that you *should* know all the answers and all the best methods of teaching and parenting. But if you can just relax, pay attention to your cooking or driving, listen to your daughter's questions, and answer them sincerely, chances are your daughter will appreciate your support, even if the information has to be revised or added to at a later time.

Listening Is the Key

Listening is the key ingredient in any communication process. Careful listening, in general, involves two important elements.

First, you must be attentive to what the person is saying without jumping ahead to what you want to say. Second, listening gives you time to tailor your responses to specific questions, comments, or emotional content. When you do these two things, your daughter is more likely to be open to what you have to say because she feels you have taken the time to really listen to her. This is especially true for conversations with your daughter about her menstrual concerns, fears, and problems. Remember, too, that you shouldn't feel guilty about giving a less than thorough explanation. This will not be the last conversation the two of you will have on the subject. Daughters are actually rather patient when mothers stay honest.

You may find it difficult to listen to all the little details that eventually lead to your daughter's menstruation question. Here is a typical example of how your listening skills may be challenged.

As Joan was preparing dinner, her eleven-year-old daughter, Lauren, told her this story: "Alissa and I were going to the gym. We passed by the new teacher, Mr. Simmons, on our way. Breann and Chelsea were already running laps. They can do more laps than even the boys in class. Jessie and Fernando challenged them last week, but Breann and Chelsea beat them. Anyway, Alissa said she needed to stop in the bathroom. I told her that we would be late and we would get in trouble. Alissa said she had to go because she had serious business that was personal. She wanted me to go with her. I told her that she should hold it until we had been to class, and then she could get permission from Mr. Glenn to go to the bathroom. She said she was going anyway. I decided to go with her and let Mr. Glenn get mad. When we got to the bathroom, Alissa opened her backpack and took out a pad. She said, 'I have to change this.' I was shocked. I didn't know that Alissa had started her period. Mom, what am I supposed to do when I get my period? Mr. Glenn made us take two more laps because we were late. That's not fair. The boys don't have to change pads. They don't give us time to even go to the bathroom just to pee, much less change pads. I felt sorry for Alissa. She didn't really feel like running the two extra laps. But, she ran them rather than tell Mr. Glenn. I wouldn't tell him, either. I'm glad I went with her even though I had to run the extra laps. It's just not fair!"

Listening to this story was a juggling act for Joan. After Lauren finished talking, Joan wasn't sure if she had listened carefully enough to her daughter's story for cues about how Lauren was feeling about menstruation—since, she simultaneously prepared dinner. She was also busy making mental notes about what she should ask her daughter later so she could better understand her. Joan was able to re-focus her attention on Lauren and hear that she was expressing some of her fears about menstruating and having to change her pad at school. Joan simply asked Lauren, "What do you think you can do when you have to change pads at school?" Lauren explored this while Joan continued preparing dinner. There was also a seed planted in Joan's mind to check out how Lauren's school responds to girls' need to change pads at school. She was sure that Lauren could handle changing pads if she had a friendly environment. However, Alissa's extra laps made Joan wonder about that environment.

Spontaneous questions and conversations make teaching easy. However, through your listening, you may realize that questions and conversations do not pop up automatically. You may need to begin conversations and know that your daughter is listening even though she appears indifferent and preoccupied. You can also engage in activities with her that address particular issues.

Here are some sample activities or ice breakers that promote communication about menstruation and body image. These activities have worked for mothers regardless of whether or not their daughters asked questions. Notice that each of these ice breakers is designed to present a small piece of information about menstruation, rather than the whole menstrual process in the one Big Talk format. Some activities may work better than others for you and your daughter.

Ice Breakers: Activities to Promote Communication

- Choose some of the stories in earlier chapters to read together. As your daughter matures, you may want to select other stories that will be of particular interest to her as she gains more experience with menstruation. (Remember that this is a process.)

- When your daughter is studying menstruation in school, suggest that the two of you read the course materials together. You may want to examine all the materials that are used in menstruation education by going to the school and asking to read them. Meeting with the teacher and learning what is being presented enables you to reinforce the points that you want your daughter to understand. Most teachers welcome questions from caring mothers.

- Make flash cards of vocabulary words related to menstruation. Words may come from school material or from the Glossary in the back of this book. If another adult in the house besides you is receptive to the idea, your daughter might use the flash cards with that person to test his or her knowledge about menstruation. Young girls love to be teachers and test the knowledge of adults.

- Encourage Girl Scout, Campfire or other club leaders to give instructions about appropriate ways to handle menstruation on camp outings, swimming activities, and overnight retreats. This cuts down fears about being unprepared or making mistakes. It also lets girls know that leaders are not ashamed to talk about menstruation and are available to them should they need help.

- Tell your own story of menstruation to your daughter or let her read the story you wrote. You can also collect menstruation stories from other adult women in the family. The women can tell or let your daughter read their stories.

- Brainstorm what to do if your daughter gets her period in different places. Start with school. Let her name all the possible places she could start her period, and then role play what she might say and do. Include as many places as your daughter can name. This helps you and your daughter practice problem solving and will probably result in some laughter, which always helps these conversations.

The Challenge: You Are Ready, But Your Daughter Is Not

You may be ready to meet the challenge of teaching menstruation only to find your daughter is a reluctant learner. In other words, *She's not interested!* There are legitimate reasons why your daughter may resist communicating about menstruation. Some daughters are hesitant to talk about menstruation because it is a strange sounding, unknown process, and they feel self-conscious about their abilities to handle the new responsibilities and expectations.

Other daughters decide at the first hint of adolescent development that, because she does not want her body to change, it won't, regardless of information to the contrary. They use magical thinking to excuse themselves from learning about anything that they believe could not happen to them. They may be determined to control their body and believe that they will not menstruate. Until a daughter is ready to let go of this thinking, she will be a most hesitant learner. Some daughters hang on to this myth of control until they actually start menstruating. Other girls are so determined not to mature or gain weight that they become anorexic as a way of avoiding it. Some exercise excessively or train in athletics or dance as a means of resistance to menstruation. These last examples are rare, but serious. If you suspect anorexia or extreme fear of menstruation, then contact your pediatrician health care provider immediately.

Another reason your daughter might be a reluctant learner is if she has been sexually abused, inappropriately touched, physically abused, or has experienced other body traumas. Whenever you approach the subject of menstruation, it may trigger memories that cloud your daughter's ability to process this new information about her body. You and your daughter might need to seek help from counselors, physicians, social workers, psychologists, or other professionals to help guide you through another step in the trauma-healing process for you and your daughter.

Dialogues about menstruation should be separated from talks about sexual activity. The emotionally loaded area of sex tends to overshadow the subject of menstruation, and both girls and their mothers find themselves overwhelmed. The media is no help in this area. Films, TV, and popular music make sex graphic and visible, while menstruation remains invisible. Your daughter may ignore menstruation just as the media does, if she is not encouraged to have a dialogue with you about it.

If you have trouble talking with your daughter about other things, talking about menstruation will not come easily. You and your daughter may have had hassles and trouble communicating about school, grades, clothes, friends, honesty, or chores. Before you can talk about menstruation, you need to build bridges and establish new ways of communicating. If you feel like a stone wall has developed between the two of you, invest the time it takes to improve your rapport with your daughter. Practice your listening skills. With courage, patience and motivation, mothers and daughters can learn new ways to talk to one another that enable both of them to be both honest and respectful. If the communication between the two of you doesn't appear to be getting better after approximately six months of effort on your part, then it is time to ask for help. Talk with your friends, adult family members, pediatrician, your health care provider, Marriage, Family, and Child Counselor, school psychologist, or pastor.

Since there are many legitimate reasons why daughters are unwilling learners about menstruation, you may need extra help in trying to get past such a stone wall. The following open-ended questions are designed to encourage a dialogue with your daughter about menstruation. I assume that, at first, most conversations with your daughter will actually be more like a monologue in which you will be the only one talking. Therefore, these questions are intended to get the ball rolling so that your daughter will feel more relaxed about discussing menstruation with you.

Questions to Encourage Dialogues About Menstruation

- I'm craving chocolate like mad today. This usually means that I'm going to start my period in a few days. I wonder how you'll know when you will start your period. What do you imagine?

- When I was your age, my mother was embarrassed to talk about menstruation. I don't feel embarrassed to talk with you about menstruation. Could it be that my mother's embarrassment skipped my generation and was passed on directly to you? How are you and grandmother alike and different?

- We're headed to the lake for our vacation. I think we should take some pads for you in case you should start your period. Is there room in your luggage for them?

- How are you feeling about the possibility of getting your period sometime soon?

- I bought a new book about menstruation. It has some diagrams showing the cycle of menstruation and some interesting stories. I'd like to show you the book and talk about it before you go to bed tonight. What time would be best for you?

- I've noticed that you have been in a quiet (crabby, sad, sensitive) mood this afternoon. Is there something going on to make you feel this way?

After you begin with the open-ended questions and continue to talk about menstruation, your daughter will open up. Then the questions that your daughter wants answered will start to surface. She may not actually ask her questions in a straightforward manner; however, if you listen you will hear them. Do you remember the questions that you wanted to ask your mother, but didn't think you could? Think about those questions. Your daughter may have many of the same ones.

Here are some questions that your daughter may want to ask you:

"When did you start to grow breasts (boobs)?"
"Did the boys or girls make fun of you because of your breasts?"
"Mom, does this really happen to you? How often?"
"Who told you about periods?"
"How do you feel when you are having your period?"
"Can you show me your ovaries?"
"When did you start having a period?"

Go ahead and answer these questions, even if your daughter never asks them. She is curious, but may be too embarrassed to ask you.

Following are activities to help stimulate continued dialogues with your daughter as her menarche approaches.

Activities to Stimulate Dialogues

- Share some of the Premenarche stories from Chapter One. Start with the stories of young girls and ask your daughter if she feels like any of these girls. Also, use the reflection questions when appropriate.

- Ask another woman (an adult woman friend, aunt, grandmother), to tell her menstruation story to your daughter.

- Collect menstruation stories from the women in your family. Let your daughter help edit them.

- Take your daughter to a lingerie department. Check out bras for yourself. This might lead to some talk about breast development and checking out beginner bras for your daughter.

- Tell your daughter about your own breast development and about buying your first bra. Such stories usually produce some laughter as well as provide information for your daughter.

Learning From Other Mothers

Professional teachers often meet together to share ideas, to talk over frustrations, and to support each other. We encourage you to meet and talk with other mothers who also need to tell their daughters about menstruation. Discuss some of the activities in this chapter with each other, share your experiences of doing the activities with your daughters, or come up with additional ice breakers you might try.

Borrowing another mother's daughter to do some of these activities can also be helpful in gaining the courage to talk with your own daughter. A school counselor met with some mothers and their thirteen-year-old daughters. She paired the mothers with each other's daughters, gave each pair a magazine and said, "Imagine that you are an anthropologist from another planet. This magazine is your source of information about the females on planet Earth. Review this magazine and be ready to give your anthropological report in fifteen minutes."

The atmosphere was electric as these teams of amateur anthropologists—comprised of women and girls who weren't related to each other—went to work. Mothers and daughters were free to talk openly since they did not hook into old fears, arguments, or attitudes that they often experienced with their own mothers or daughters. The reports back to the group provided both mothers and daughters relevant information for their discussions on the way home, the next day, and even weeks later.

Do not be discouraged if you approach other mothers and find that they are reluctant to talk about menstruation. Get together with those who are willing to talk and share ideas. Mothers are hesitant to talk about menstruation for the same reasons that daughters are. Our culture and individual histories silence many women. Your desire to have your daughter incorporate menstruation into her life as a natural, healthy body function without shame and embarrassment will motivate you to give up your own silence and to connect with other mothers who have the courage to talk with you and their daughters about menstruation.

I haven't included Things To Do or Things To Think About, since this chapter is comprised mainly of activities. Remember keep talking. Your daughter will be listening.

Chapter 9

Talk with the men in your life about menstruation

Whether presenting lectures or just talking about this book, I continually hear from fathers, "Hey, what about us?" More fathers than I thought are also teaching their daughters about menstruation. Not only are fathers talking with their daughters about menstruation, they are often the ones whom their daughters come to when their first period begins.

I wrote this chapter to encourage fathers to talk with their daughters (and sons) about menstruation. Like mothers, fathers can practice with other fathers, and with spouses, until they are more relaxed and confident talking about both the facts and the feelings associated with menstruation. I not only recommend that fathers use the activities, suggestions, and information in this book to help them prepare for conversations with their daughters, but that they read the stories written by the young girls and women throughout the book. Most men want to know how women experience menstruation and are curious to learn more. Fathers may want to identify those stories which best illustrate their own daughter's attitude toward menstruation.

Fathers and Menstruation

Fathers are important people in their daughters' lives for a variety of reasons. With more mothers working, there is an increased chance that the father may be the one who is home when the daughter begins her menstrual cycle. In addition, more and more daughters are living with their fathers and away from their mothers, either full time or part time, because of separation, divorce, death, or other circumstances.

Daughters often protest that they do not want their fathers to know that they have started their periods. But fathers must accept that their daughters are growing up, and daughters must be aware of the fact that their fathers are informed about menstruation and can provide help and assistance when needed.

Why is it so important for fathers to be involved? When a father is able to talk openly with his daughter about menstruation, it sends her the positive message that this normal female function is accepted by men, and is not something to be ashamed of or embarrassed about. By discussing menstruation in a respectful and straightforward way with his adolescent daughter, a father helps her develop a healthy attitude about her body and her relationship to men. Of course, the more involved a father is in his daughter's life, and the closer his relationship to her, the easier it will be for him to talk with her about menstruation and the other physical and emotional changes she is experiencing. And the more easily daughters are able to talk with their fathers about menstruation and adolescence, the more comfortable they will be later about discussing sexual issues.

I have heard many wonderful stories of the ways fathers and daughters handled menarche: while out on the trail—camping, hiking, or cycling; when daughters are visiting fathers, and no one else is around. Daughters hint to their fathers about what they think has occurred. Fathers occasionally must improvise the information and sanitary supplies. Some daughters blush while their fathers recount these "adventures," but the father's face always beams with pride. As the girls watch their fathers' faces, they begin to smile, a smile that only a daughter can have for her father.

Other memorable experiences include fathers who do something special for their daughter's menarche: going out for a celebratory dinner with her; giving her balloons, flowers, or an appropriate gift. Such celebrations leave daughters with a lasting impression of feeling special and acknowledged as a maturing young woman. Girls may moan and groan at the time, but within a few years they will treasure their fathers' time and recognition.

Many women remember that once they began to menstruate, their fathers treated them differently. Physical nurturing was abruptly cut off, as fathers refrained from hugging or kissing, or having their daughters sit on their laps. As girls, these women were puzzled and hurt by the change in their relationships with their fathers. From a nine, ten, or thirteen-year-old girl's point of view, she may be menstruating, but she doesn't think of herself as a grown woman. She is still "daddy's girl," who wants to be seen as growing up, but not so grown up that she cannot continue to have his hugs and kisses.

Many fathers believe that once their daughters begin to menstruate, they want to be treated like women. After all, preteen and teenage girls do say this at least a million times to their fathers and mothers, don't they? However, what girls say and what they actually want from parents can be completely different. Girls want to be acknowledged as looking and behaving like young women, but this doesn't mean that they want to give up being affectionate with their fathers. Fathers, on the other hand, not only want to respect their daughter's stated wish to be treated as a woman, they're also afraid of being too physically affectionate. They know that it is not acceptable to be sexual with their daughters, and one of the best ways to ensure that no one thinks they are acting inappropriately is to refrain from any physical contact with her. Unfortunately, when a father does this, his daughter misunderstands his actions and believes that he is not interested in her anymore. This is a difficult situation for fathers. It is vitally important that they continue to be physically affectionate with their daughters in appropriate ways and, at the same time, to acknowledge that their daughters are growing into mature females. Fathers who make a conscious effort to stay involved with their daughters during this time will contribute not only to a lasting father-daughter relationship, but to the daughter's overall trust in men and belief in herself.

I cannot overemphasize the value of a father's involvement with his preteen and teenage daughters. These adolescent years are difficult as young girls struggle to define their place in the world and the place of males in their lives. Daughters can be loving and gentle one moment, and then turn on their fathers with disgust and indignation the next. Even though these incidents are distressing, daughters continue to profit from their father's input and involvement. Her father's guidance and interest in her life are remembered and valued for years to come. If fathers doubt their importance, then think about how fondly adult women often speak of their fathers. A father's belief in his daughter helps give her determination to reach for her goals.

It is truly amazing how very different father-daughter conversations are from mother-daughter ones. Fathers and daughters talk about diverse subjects; they bicker, disagree, argue, and become side-tracked into what appears to be irrelevant issues. Many times, a father will suggest to his daughter that she do (or not do) something, and she willingly accepts his advice. For mothers, this can be exasperating, especially since you talked with your daughter hundreds of times about the same thing to no avail. Her father tells her once, and she acts as if this is the first time anyone has made the suggestion. Why this happens is open to various interpretations; maybe she finally saw the logic in what was proposed, maybe her father said it in a way that she could understand, or maybe she wanted to please him. No one can ever say for certain. This is the relationship between fathers and daughters during adolescence: frustrating, teasing, and irritating each other at one moment, loving, respecting, and adoring each other the next.

Teaching Brothers About Menstruation

Brothers also need education about menstruation. Many younger brothers are too uncomfortable to admit that they are lacking in information. And older brothers who know the facts may still need to be taught to respect their sisters and to be more sensitive.

At some point, young boys usually want to learn about menstruation. Since menstruation doesn't happen to their bodies, boys are less frightened of the unknown and, therefore, normally ask more direct questions. Their straightforward questions can be alarming to both parents. Whenever sons ask questions, it is wise to answer as directly as you can.

When your young daughter is approaching menarche, I recommend that both parents talk with her brothers, older and younger. Brothers six and under may not be interested in an explanation about menstruation. If they show no concern, then they are probably not ready. Older brothers are most likely curious and have questions. Parents may feel more comfortable bringing up this topic when both are present, or each may want to talk individually to their sons. It is important to answer your son's questions honestly and to repeat the information in many different ways as the days and years go by.

Explanations that are short and succinct are best for young sons. For example,

Your sister is growing up. She is becoming a strong, healthy young woman. Before long, she will begin to menstruate, which only females do. Females menstruate because they have a uterus inside their bodies. It is in the uterus where a baby grows. Once a girl reaches puberty, her body produces a lining of tissues inside her uterus. Then about once a month, the lining is shed as menstrual blood through her vagina. Males do not have uteruses or vaginas and, therefore, cannot become pregnant. Menstruation is the body's sign to the girl that she can become pregnant. When girls begin to menstruate, they must take care of their bodies in special ways. Sometimes boys who are uninformed or misinformed about menstruation make fun of girls who they think are menstruating. This is something that we do not want you to do to your sister or any other girl. This teasing behavior may look harmless to you, but it can hurt a girl's feelings, plus the teasing makes you look uninformed about this normal female body function.

This is usually enough for the beginning discussion about menstruation. If, however, your son asks questions, then answer him as simply as possible. Let him know that you will answer any of his questions, and that you will talk more with him about menstruation.

Older brothers are often misinformed about menstruation and remain misinformed until they have their first serious girlfriend. She is the one who teaches him about menstruation. For the mothers, think about whether or not you educated your boyfriends. For the fathers, think about what your parents taught you about menstruation and what your girlfriends taught you.

Now you may think, "What is wrong with this? This is a normal, special, intimate, trust-building relationship." And I agree; however, there are many years in between first hearing about menstruation and becoming sensitive to what it means in a woman's life. Boys often tease girls because of their own ignorance and a desire to appear more knowledgeable than they are. Girls' feelings get hurt; they become embarrassed or angry, and they often strike back with demeaning comments, insults, or incorrect information. So don't wait until your son has a girlfriend. He needs to know about menstruation now so he won't tease his sister or other girls. Just begin the dialogue and keep it going. Older brothers tend to act as if they know more about menstruation than they actually do. Just keep talking and they will listen.

Most older brothers tease their sisters about practically everything. No surprise here! However, once younger sisters approach menses, they are less likely to tolerate their brothers' jokes and prodding. Some daughters speak up, while others become depressed and withdraw from the family. The best way to handle this situation is by discussing with your son the way he felt when his body changed. He may need to be reminded that his feet and hands grew before his body caught up; that his voice changed, cracked, squeaked; that he grew pubic and underarm hair, worried about body odor and the size of his penis; that he was sensitive, moody and didn't like to be teased. And then he started comparing himself to other boys and worrying what girls thought about him. Explain to your son that the family did its best to be understanding while he got used to living with the changes. You are merely requesting that he do the same for his younger sister.

Younger sisters may be embarrassed if their older brothers talk about menstruation. Yet, by encouraging your son to have a short talk with his sister, both will feel closer. Brothers will also be less likely to tease their sisters and other girls. Also, suggest that your son and daughter talk about practical ways he can be helpful to her; i.e., if she unexpectedly begins her period and needs money for pads or tampons, or help getting home. This partnership can provide the emotional bond that sisters and brothers both crave and deserve.

I encourage both the women and the men in your family to read the stories in this chapter. The first story is written by a father whose daughter had her first menstrual period while they were together. The other stories were written by men recalling their first memories of menstruation, how they learned (or didn't learn!) about it, and how this knowledge—or lack of it—affected their lives.

From the Male Point of View

"My First Time—(and Ashlea's, too)" • William, Age 43

"Oh God! I never bargained for this!" was my first, absolutely secret, hidden, internal reaction. My verbal, and visible, external response actually went something like, "Oh, we'll have to call your mother and tell her the big news. But first let's go over to that 7-11 we passed and get you the stuff you'll need."

I was in the middle of Iowa with my two daughters on RAGBRAI, an annual, week-long, organized, cross-Iowa, bike ride with thousands of participants. I had done it the previous year with just my eldest daughter, Ashlea, then 11, on a tandem. This year she was 12 and on her own bike. At night, she shared a tent with her 10-year-old sister, Jennifer, who was on the tandem with me. Ashlea had completed much longer and hillier rides than any day scheduled in Iowa, so I was pretty sure she could make it. I hoped that her comments about discomfort on the bike the past two days resulted only from the difference between its seat and the tandem's. The alternative was much more daunting.

And "it" happened. She brought the evidence to me after the girls showered at the end of a long day. The bloody glop in her chamois-lined cycling shorts showed me she had gotten her first period. (I only learned later what menarche means.)

"Where was her mother when we needed her? How come this kind of thing always happens to me? What do I do now?" Those are the kinds of (self-centered) questions that instantly ran through my mind. But luckily for Ashlea (and my reputation as a "Daddy") I kept my cool and took her to a nearby convenience store. They had all the stuff for "it" in a section of the store that I usually never visit. I looked at tampons, but I couldn't imagine how they could ever fit in "there." So I picked out some of the newest, most high-tech, ultra-thin pads that they sold. I figured the old thick ones would be too uncomfortable on a long bike ride. Ashlea tells me that they were "OK." She forgot the pads once a couple of evenings later and got a tampon from another woman on the ride, but couldn't insert it. When she got home, her mother "poo-poohed" those thin pads, but since has converted to them. I also looked through all the women's medicines and picked out some Midol for her. She took it a few times, probably just to humor me, but tells me she never needed it very badly.

After getting the "stuff" we seemed to need, we called her mother and told her..., a big mistake! Left home alone, and lonely, her mother felt obligated to tell all her friends the "big news." It seems that Ashlea had her first period on the very same day that her best friend, Kim did. That was sooo cute! Ashlea was really glad to come home after RAGBRAI and find out that her most intimate bodily functions were common knowledge.

"My Girlfriend Tells Me" • Blake, Age 20

Jennifer is my current girlfriend. She is much more outspoken, communicative, and older than my first girl friend, Kim. I've learned much from her through our open conversations, and I have also learned to be more observant of her behavior.

Jennifer always tells me when she is having her period. She generally feels agitated during the first few days of her period. Through observations, I've come to realize that this also serves as a warning. Anytime I've acted silly or wanted to tease her during those first days of her period, she has been irritated and snapped at me.

Jennifer often has cramps and sometimes feels sick to her stomach when she is having her period. One time I asked her how the cramps felt. She replied, "Kind of like your stomach and intestines are turning inside out." Since that conversation, I've tried to be much more conscious of my actions around her during her period. I just remind myself of bad cases of stomach flu that I've had. The pain she described sounds a lot like the pain I had. I find it remarkable that she can carry on normally with that kind of pain each month.

I talked to Jennifer about the use of tampons. I asked her what it felt like to walk around with a tampon in her vagina for hours. To my amazement, she said that she really can't feel the tampon. She sometimes forgets that she has one in her. She said some women forget they are wearing a tampon and leave it in more than a day without changing it. I learned that this can be dangerous. It can even lead to Toxic Shock Syndrome. This makes women extremely sick, and in extreme cases can lead to death. I don't want Jennifer to get this. I jokingly told her that I thought her cramps were good because they constantly remind her of her period and to change her tampon. She didn't think my joke was funny and gave me a wicked glare.

According to Jennifer, her monthly period is something she has learned to get used to. As far as she told me, the only drawbacks she feels about her menstrual cycle are the severe cramps she gets, and men who accuse her of "being on the rag" when she is not behaving the way they want her to behave. Jennifer and I have had many conversations about menstruation. Since we can talk about a subject which is often taboo between males and females, we feel strong enough to talk about anything.

"Dad, What's A Period?" • Joshua, Age 18

Silence...It was a warm day in May and the quiet hum of nature was in the air. As a cool breeze passed over the lake, the voices of two males could be heard chatting in the quiet.

"What a big fish. Too bad it got away, Billy."

"Dad, what's a period?"

"What?"

"A period. What is it?"

Billy, what ever made you ask such a question?"

"I saw a movie at school and it was about growing up. My teacher told me that only boys could see this movie. The girls saw another movie. My friend's sister said that she saw a movie about girls having periods."

As I turned to look at my father, he was looking down and could not answer. Finally he said, "Did you ask your mother about this?"

"No, why should I? Don't you know what a period is?"

"Well," Dad began, "a period, I think is what a woman gets during a cycle that's called menstruation. She gets this period every month. During this cycle some women, like your mother, tend to get a bit on the moody side. That's when flowers are helpful, son. You may also notice that we dine out during one week every month. To tell you the truth, I really didn't know what a period was until I was in high school. And on top of that, I had to learn about it the hard way. I had to ask the girls I dated. I believe that if periods were not such a personal subject for women, men would understand women more during that certain time of month. Men just need to be told more about menstruation from a woman's point of view. Anyway, is that all you want to know?"

"No," I said. "What is it really?"

With a gentle smile Dad replied, "That's really all you have to know for now, but if you want more information, please ask your mother. Now, let's get back to fishing."

"OK, Dad."

During this short fishing trip, I got to share some quality time with my Dad. I also learned what precious little information it had taken him a lifetime to know. He was still uncomfortable with the subject, and I will need more information to pass on to my son.

"Girls Go Through A Lot more Than Boys" • Nicholas, Age 19

Menstruation is something that most guys find difficult to talk about. We especially do not understand the mood and attitude changes of women.

When I first encountered menstruation, I was in the 7th grade. I did not learn about menstruation from my parents or any adult. As a young boy hanging around with other boys, menstruation appeared to be something funny. We used it as something to ridicule and make fun of girls. Although I didn't quite understand what it was, we boys used to say our teachers (both men and women) were "on the rag" when they were being mean or moody. Even though I didn't understand what it meant, I knew that everyone (both boys and girls) used it as a form of a bad word. I didn't really know what being "on the rag" meant, or what it had to do with a period. After a while, I figured out that a period occurred once a month and girls avoided wearing white during this time. I remember that at lunch other boys used to joke about pouring fruit juice on girls' seats so when they sat down they would stain their pants. Fortunately, we talked more than we acted.

The first encounter I had with the seriousness of menstruation was when I was in 9th grade. I was about half an hour late to class. I was walking to my class when I heard a girl crying and a female teacher comforting her. The teacher said, "It is natural for this to happen. One can't exactly know when it will happen." At this point, I really didn't know what they were talking about. I did notice that the girl was upset and crying. Then the girl said, "It's embarrassing. Everyone saw and I have no control over it." This stayed with me all day. I thought perhaps she had tripped or burped or something like that. I could not understand why someone would get so upset. It did not occur to me until about a month later in health class when I learned about the female reproductive system and how the uterus cleans itself each month. After this health lesson, it was no longer funny to think about staining girls' pants with fruit juice.

As I entered high school, the subject of menstruation was more serious. At home, no one really talked about or mentioned menstruation. I would never have known about it if it was not for school. Most guys used this natural occurrence as an excuse to explain why girls had short tempers. I had a real close female friend who trusted and confided in me. She would tell me everything. I learned from her that some girls take birth control pills so they can avoid cramps and regulate their periods. She told me about her pain and discomfort during her period. She also told me that she gets moody when she is on her period. She even avoids some activities because she cannot predict when she will get her period and how she will feel.

Girls go through a lot more than boys. In fact, girls are probably tougher than boys when you see how much they go through with menstruation. When I think of this, I'm glad I'm not a girl. It will not be easy for me to explain menstruation to my son. I will probably explain the details of menstruation in medical terms. I would also remind him that menstruation is not something that girls have by choice. It is, therefore, something that he should not use to make fun of girls. I wish I had not made fun of girls for this natural occurrence when I was in junior high school.

"Why Do Girls Have Little Dots?" • Marcus, Age 24

One time when I was about seven, I walked into a room just as Aunt Rose was telling Grandmother about some rather strong cramps she was having. When Aunt Rose finished what she was saying, I told them about a cramp I got that day while swimming. As soon as they both controlled their laughter, Aunt Rose told me that I should have taken some Midol (a medicine used to relieve menstrual cramps). I told her that I did not have any at the time, but that I would remember to take some with me when I went to the pool again. Afterwards, Grandmother explained to me that Aunt Rose was talking about cramps that only women have. Instead of asking more questions, I just said, "Oh!"

Later my mother talked to me about menstruation. She used the word, "period." Based on the only definition I knew for that word, I now believed that women got little black dots (.) that caused cramps.

My Uncle Mick got married when I was eight years old. A year later, Aunt Gina got pregnant. I remember hearing Aunt Gina tell Grandmother that she was glad to get a break from her period for nine months. Of course, Grandmother told Aunt Gina that there would be many other discomforts to take its place. "Aha!" I thought. Periods have something to do with having babies. I had picked up a little knowledge which suggested that I did not have to worry about this period stuff since I was a boy.

I can also remember each year that some guy would try to pull the same trick on a teacher. It always seemed to be the same type of kid, the troublesome one who was looking for a fight and trying to impress other kids. Each year this boy would slip a tampon into the teacher's desk and wait for the teacher to find it. It always turned out the same; the teacher would find the tampon, become furious, and say, "Who did this?" I never knew what the teacher was holding, but I laughed as hard as anyone else so I would not look as if I didn't know what was happening. The teacher would know exactly who did it and send that kid to see the principal. I got the impression that each time some kid would try that gag, they knew very well that they would be caught and sent to the principal. It must have been a small price to pay for entertaining the class.

Finally in the 6th grade, after seeing this tampon gag four times, I found out by accident that the thing the teacher was holding was a tampon. A friend was explaining about the trick for a guy who was absent. He said, "Damien put a tampon on Mrs. Boynton's desk." This still didn't mean much to me because I didn't know what a tampon was used for. It was, however, one more piece of information that proved useful later on.

A few weeks later, I was looking for a new bar of soap under the bathroom sink when I saw a box with "tampon" printed on it. I had never seen "tampon" written before, so it took me a few moments to sound it out and realize what it was. I was a little bit excited that I was about to know as much as most of my friends about these things. I opened the box and saw a whole bunch of those familiar wrapped tubes. I took one wrapper off. I took this cardboard tube apart and wound up being more confused than enlightened. I had no idea what this thing was for. I quickly pushed the pieces way down to the bottom of the trash can and put the box back under the sink. I figured that I might as well learn as much as I could while I was there. Next I found a box with "maxi pad" on it. Before I opened the box, I tried to imagine what a "maxi pad" was going to look like. I opened that box and found some long, oval, soft things. I thought about Alice getting bigger and bigger and said to myself, "Curiouser and curiouser!" (Yes, Alice in Wonderland was a favorite story, even then.)

All of the information I had stored began to come together around 7th grade. I started to take more notice of the Playtex commercials and their use of the words like, "maxi, protection, and comfort." By then, my knowledge of the subject had grown to the point where I knew a woman's period to be a pain that they got every month. It put women in a bad mood and required the use of soft padded things. What I still did not know was what the soft padded things were for, and why women had periods anyway.

After trying to watch commercials more closely to see if I could get answers, I noticed that they never really said what tampons and sanitary napkins were specifically for. I thought to myself, "deodorant commercials tell you where to spray, and soap and shampoo commercials tell you what they are and how to use them. Why don't these Playtex people show me how and where to use these pads and tubes?" When answers finally hit me, I felt very relieved and a bit smarter. I still did not know why women even had periods. This question went unanswered for months because I was too embarrassed to ask anyone.

I finally heard Grandmother use the word "menstruation" in a conversation. I was still too embarrassed to ask her about it, so I looked it up in our family medical guide. It didn't do me much good because the words were way too big, and I never had enough patience to look up all the words that I didn't know. I just decided to put the whole subject away because it would not affect me anyway, or so I thought.

When I got to high school, I had a health teacher who was comfortable talking about any subject. When we got to the part of our book that dealt with menstruation, she went ahead and explained the whole process clearly. I was thankful that finally someone would talk to me about it.

"No Fair! Candy Machines in the Girls' Bathroom" • Jeffrey, Age 18

This is my story about women, their menstruation, and how I learned about this process. I believe men should know about menstruation so that they can understand the women they love. I found out about menstruation through curiosity.

When I was seven or eight, I was with my beautiful mother. We were at a carnival. Suddenly, I really, really had to go to the bathroom. My mother did not want me to go by myself because the men's bathrooms were so crowded, and she was also afraid that I would get lost. She took me into the ladies' bathroom.

Little did she know I was about to enter the world of menstruation. When I walked out of the stall, I looked around for my mother. I couldn't find her, and I started to get real nervous. I yelled, "Mom! Mom! Where are you?" Finally, I heard a voice from the last stall. "Don't worry, Jeffrey, I'm here. Just calm down. I'll be out in a second." Even though she said she was coming, I still felt nervous remembering I was in the ladies' bathroom. Just then I heard some women's voices headed towards the bathroom. This is when I started to search for a spot to hide.

Next thing I knew, I banged my head on this large gray box on the wall. My mother was out of the stall by this time. I got up and started to look at this weird box. Then it came to me. I said, "You have a candy machine in your bathroom. No wonder the girls are always staying in the bathroom."

My mother was standing behind me with the two women who had walked in. They were giggling and my mother's face turned a little red and had a strange look on it. She grabbed my hand and we walked out the door quickly. She was quiet and then I said, "Mom, that's not fair. How come you women have a candy machine and we don't?"

She stopped, turned to me and said, "Jeff, that is not a candy machine. That is a machine made especially for women. It is a necessity and helps women deal with the pain and embarrassment of their cycles."

I didn't know what she was talking about. I could tell she was uncomfortable and didn't want to talk about it. I didn't push it. We were silent for awhile, and then we just smiled at each other and forgot about it for the time. This was just the beginning of my discovery of menstruation.

My next experience with menstruation occurred when I was about ten. I was in Mass with my family. All of a sudden, one of my sisters started complaining about cramps. I didn't know what she was talking about. I knew she didn't play any sports with us the day before, so how could she have cramps? I heard my Mom say to my Dad, "Her monthly visit has come." The next thing I knew, my Mom and sister went outside. I thought to myself, "Why does she get to leave Mass just because she has cramps? My legs are twice as sore as hers, but I am still kneeling here praying, and she's out the door without a single prayer." I turned to my father and asked him if I could leave for awhile because my cramps were pretty bad, too. He whispered, "I'm sure you don't have the cramps your sister has." I still didn't understand, but I let it go. I sat through the rest of Mass with a puzzled look on my face trying to understand what he meant.

There is another experience that sticks out in my mind about menstruation. I overheard my sisters arguing angrily. My oldest sister, Mary, turned to Ann and said, "What's wrong with you, PMS?" They kept arguing. For some reason, that stood out in my mind. After the argument was over, I walked over to Ann and asked her, "What is PMS? What does it mean?"

Ann turned to me and said, "Look, Jeff, you don't need to know." Her response made me even more curious. I kept asking her and she wouldn't tell me. I finally bugged her enough. She grabbed both my shoulders, looked me straight in the eye, and said, "PMS, Jeff, stands for 'Putting up with Men's Shit!' Now, leave me alone." As she walked away, I just looked at her. She was so serious and sure of herself, I believed her.

The information Ann gave me surfaced, again, two weeks later at a wedding reception. I was standing in line waiting for a glass of punch. I overheard two ladies talking. One of the ladies said to the other in a low voice, "What's the matter with Rachel, lately? Must be PMS." I got excited when I heard this. Now I knew what they were talking about. It was not a secret code anymore. I had broken the code. I was so anxious to get to my sister and let her know, that I got out of line and looked for her. When I finally found her, she was with some older girl cousins. I kept trying to interrupt her. Finally, she said, "What is it, Jeff?" I looked at her with a smile on my face and said, "You see, Rachel, over there?" They all looked where I pointed. Ann said, "Yeah, what about her?"

"That lady has PMS." Ann and our cousins looked at me in amazement. Then one of our cousins said to me, "How do you know about PMS?" I answered with a sort of cockiness and confidence, "Oh, that's easy. Ann's been Putting up with Men's Shit for weeks."

There was a huge roar of laughter. I didn't understand what was so funny. All I knew was that for a moment, I was the life of the party. After they all stopped laughing, they looked at me with red faces and just shook their heads. Every time they looked at me that day, they would start to smile and then giggle. I didn't know what was going on, but I enjoyed the attention.

These are just a few of the early experiences with menstruation that I remember. Through all of these experiences, I learned a little about the female and her cycle. Each time I would gather the knowledge from past experiences and put it together like a puzzle. I have learned a lot through the years. I am pretty sure I now know most of the game plan when it comes to menstruation. Having a mother and two sisters who are open helped me along the way to understanding things that were at first confusing. My curiosity about menstruation has caused me several moments of embarrassment. My knowledge, however, about women and this important function helps me to be more sensitive and closer to women I love. That's important to me.

Jeffrey states that his mother and two sisters were "open" with him about menstruation, and yet his story reveals just the opposite! Every time he requested information from either his mother or sisters, he was met with silence, anger, hostility, or ridicule! Women and girls also need to take some responsibility for men's and boys' ignorance and insensitivity concerning menstruation. Jeffrey's story is a perfect example of a young boy who wanted to know the facts about menstruation, but was unable to get them from any member of his family. Not only do women need to be open with brothers and sons, but if girls don't want to get teased by boys, shouldn't sisters and mothers be equally respectful and not use such phrases as, "putting up with men's shit?" While such an expression may be funny to women, isn't it as offensive as "on the rag?"

Things to Think About

- What do these young men still need to know about menstruation?

- How did these young men treat young women in relation to menstruation?

- How do the young girls treat the boys? Think about Jeffrey's story and his sisters teasing him. How do you feel about this and their expression for "PMS?" Is this as offensive to men as "on the rag" is to women? Why so?

- What was sad in these stories? Why so?

- How do you think boys should be educated about menstruation?

- What role should fathers, mothers, sisters, older brothers play in educating boys about menstruation?

Chapter 10

Menarche is a time
to celebrate

Menarche is a visible rite of passage for young girls. The menstrual flow is a concrete marker of changes in a girl's body which allow her to produce the next generation. It is a momentous event that is certainly cause for celebration. Some cultures have a formal ceremony for this transition. In such ceremonies, the girl comes to the event as a child and leaves it as a woman. After the ceremony, everyone is expected to treat the girl as a young woman.

There are two types of menarcheal rites-of-passage which anthropologists and other researchers have identified in cultures around the world. The first type involves joyous celebrations of fertility and acceptance of the initiate into adult society. The second involves physical mutilation or painful rituals of degradation and coercion by the society.

One of the most beautiful ceremonies is the Navajo Kinaaldá. It is also one of their most important religious rites. There is a five-day and night celebration. The menarcheal girl goes into seclusion, where she is instructed by women about her new responsibilities of hygiene and behavior as a menstruating female of the tribe. She learns about the honorable purpose of menstruation and her place in the perpetuation of her tribe's people and their way of life. After the girl has learned her lessons to the satisfaction of the women of the tribe, celebrations and feasts commemorate her acceptance of, and the tribe's recognition of, her new valuable status.

Another Native American tribe, the Mescalero Apache, has a single celebration for all girls who began menstruation during the last year. The girls are recognized during four days of public ceremonies, followed by another four days of private ceremonies. There is also feasting, present giving and dancing.

In different areas of India, the menarcheal girl is secluded from family and friends. During this time, she bathes using ceremonial oils. After the seclusion there is a banquet for relatives, friends, and neighbors who bring presents to the girl. Usually, one of the gifts is a full-length sari worn only by Indian women which replaces her short child's dress.

Many traditional Japanese families inform their relatives and friends by symbols, rather than by elaborate celebration. There is a Japanese custom that the parents of the menarcheal girl prepares a meal for invited guests and places a fresh or candied fruit with stem and leaves still attached on the main food tray. The significance of the gesture is understood, and the girl is accepted into her new status in the family.

There are many more examples of menstrual rites-of-passage, both beautiful and horrific. In this book, I have chosen to ignore those that are physically and emotionally damaging and degrading to the girl in particular and women in general. If you are interested in learning more about the history of menstrual rites and taboos and their place in different societies, *Red Flower, Rethinking Menstruation*, by Dena Taylor, and *The Curse, A Cultural History of Menstruation*, by Delaney, Lupton & Toth are excellent sources.

In our modern secular culture, rites-of-passage are not regarded as important times for celebrations, and menarche, in particular, has been overlooked and relegated to an unobserved and unspoken occurrence in a young girl's life. I believe that there is a great deal to be said for observing rites-of-passage in general. Every major religion features a ceremony honoring the passage from childhood to adulthood. The ceremony informs the individual that he or she now occupies a new status in the community and that this new status comes with responsibilities, but also with specific privileges. The ceremony notifies the community that this individual has moved into a new and valued role. In the Jewish faith, girls and boys at age thirteen celebrate their Bat Mitzvah or Bar Mitzvah. This celebration publicly recognizes the thirteen-year-old, and he or she accepts a new and important role in sustaining the Jewish faith. In Christianity, Confirmation rites fulfill the same purpose. For other individuals, graduation from school or an academy or training program publicly signifies a change in status. The common thread is that the individuals perceive that they are changed, and that the community acknowledges them as changed and more valuable members. I believe that even without these public rites-of-passage there are many life transitions and events which deserve to be commemorated privately within the family. Menarche is just one of them.

Since in our modern secular culture we have no public rite-of-passage for menstruation, our challenge as parents is to create an appropriate personal or family celebration which signifies the passage from one life stage, childhood, to the next stage, adolescence. I use the word "adolescence," rather than "womanhood" or "adulthood," because young girls at menarche know that they are not yet adults. They do not have all the rights, privileges, and responsibilities of adult women. In fact, many girls become insulted if you tell them they have reached "womanhood" simply because they have begun to menstruate. Young girls know that they are capable of reproducing, but also that they are not yet perceived or accepted as adults by society's laws.

There are increasing numbers of parents and families who acknowledge that when a girl develops the capacity to reproduce, there should be a recognition of this, and so they provide her with a personal or familial celebration. I hope as you and your daughter read about these celebrations, you'll be inspired to create one of your own. Later in the chapter, I'll provide some suggestions that may help you decide how to mark this important event in your daughter's life.

Celebrations of Menarche

In the story in Chapter Four, *I Don't Want a Party*, Sarita was anxious because she feared that her mother might have a party to celebrate her menarche. Sarita was certain that she would die from embarrassment if her mother gave her a party. Would she really have been embarrassed, or would she have been happy that her mother provided a celebration? Like most girls today, Sarita did not have a framework in which to imagine a celebration for her menarche.

Stories about menarche celebrations are not plentiful in our communities. Why not? If menarche is a rite-of-passage from girlhood to sexual maturity, and since it is a milestone of development, why aren't we celebrating it? Perhaps, like Sarita, we have no blueprint for how a menarche party might be organized. Hallmark is not yet selling cards saying, "Congratulations on your menarche." Despite the fact that devising a suitable, yet unique, celebration for menarche takes time and thought, I am aware of a number of families who have taken it upon themselves to come up with their own celebrations for their daughter. I think you'll be encouraged to have your own menarche event as you hear from these families.

Frank and His Daughter, Alissa: A Very Special Dinner

Frank, a divorced dad who has joint custody of his daughter, Alissa, told Alissa at least a year before her menarche that he wanted to take her out to a special dinner—at the restaurant of her choice—when she got her first period. When she was about nine years old, he had made sure that they discussed what menstruation was all about and what Alissa should expect. He had also purchased menstrual supplies and kept them in Alissa's bathroom in case she should get her period for the first time when she was at his house. Although Alissa had also discussed menstruation with her mother, it made her feel more comfortable to know that her father was prepared for the upcoming event should it happen when she was with him.

Frank and Alissa had fun talking about which restaurant Alissa would choose for her celebration. She loves Japanese food, and Frank promised to take her to an elegant Japanese restaurant where the waitresses wear beautiful kimonos and where you can sit on the floor in a private, authentically decorated Japanese room. They were both looking forward to this time. It was also a way for Frank to insure that Alissa would tell him about her first period since it was her ticket to a very special dinner.

Frank had to rearrange his schedule quickly when Alissa's menarche arrived on a Wednesday. During a steak teriyaki dinner, they talked about Alissa's birth and some other memories of her childhood. They mostly talked about the books they were reading, Alissa's soccer team, summer vacation plans, other members of the family, and what Alissa wanted for her twelfth birthday. The celebration of Alissa's menarche has helped her to share her monthly period frustrations with her father. It has also kept their communication more open. Frank says he is more sensitive to his daughter's moods and to her struggles.

Katie and Her Godmother, Mara: A Handmade Book

One of the women Katie feels the closest to is her godmother, Mara. When she got her period for the first time, Mara was the first person she called after her best friend at school. Mara told Katie she wanted to give her a gift to celebrate Katie's menarche, and the two arranged to have tea together. Over tea, Mara handed Katie a unique handmade book, the first page of which read, "Welcome to the World of Women." The rest of the book contained cartoons that poked fun at stereotypes of females of all ages. The captions in the book clearly emphasized the joy of being a female who likes and believes in herself. Mara knows that handling forty years of periods can best be done with a keen sense of humor. She told Katie about Sophia, the spirit of feminine wisdom, who Mara is certain would approve of the wisely humorous book now treasured by Katie.

Anna's Ceremonial Camping Trip

In discussing fears about how her life might change once she got her period, Anna told her mother that she didn't want to stop doing any of the activities she loved—like soccer, rollerblading, and camping trips. Her mom told her not to worry; there was no reason why Anna couldn't rollerblade, play soccer, or camp out anytime she wanted to. In fact, when Anna got her first period, her mother suggested the family go on a camping trip the following weekend to celebrate—and Anna could invite along her best friend, Tracy, as well.

The camp-out was just as much fun as always, with hikes during the day and campfires at night. Only this time, Anna's family—her mom, dad, sister, and brother—and Tracy decided to make this particular camping trip uniquely memorable. Under a star-studded sky, with roasted marshmallows in hand, they all toasted to Anna's "new status as a menstruating adolescent who is well on her way to womanhood." It will be a camping trip she'll never forget.

Cheers for those families who create celebrations for their daughters. Family celebrations make it easier for a girl to feel comfortable about this natural process that has now become part of her life.

There are also mini-celebrations of menarche. Girls call significant women in their lives and tell them that they have started their periods. The warm responses of grandmothers, aunts, and older women friends provide a sense of rejoicing that the girl has passed another milestone in her development. Imagine the telephone commercial that shows a girl on the phone:

"Hi, Grandma. Guess what? I just started my period."

"Oh, Courtney, that's wonderful! Tell me about it."

Ideas for Creating a Menarche Celebration

This last section of the book contains ideas for menarche celebrations which can be enjoyable, meaningful, and tradition building. I suggest that you begin discussion well before your daughter gets her period about what to include in the menarche-recognizing event. It is best for mother, father, and daughter to present ideas about simple ways to celebrate her upcoming menarche. My experience is that some girls are not receptive to the idea of a menarche-recognizing event. Explain to her that you know this isn't often celebrated, but you want to do somthing special for her. Keep making suggestions and, before long she'll probably agree to something, if only to get you to stop talking about it. Persist; the memories are worth it.

If your daughter begins her period before you have planned a celebration with her, you can still have a brainstorming sessions and plan a time to honor her. Older sisters, who did not have menarche commemorations, might also be included and honored as well. If appropriate, they can be acknowledged for their special roles as the "wiser" menstruating older sister.

The important aspects of the celebration are: (1) include intimate family members, relatives and friends; (2) recognize menstruation as a step towards womanhood, and (3) keep the communication channels open among family members for future discussions about dating, sexuality, and marriage. Here are a few suggestions from my twelve-year-old daughter, our family, and friends: invite family members to create poems, sketches, photograph albums, or video tapes especially for the occasion. Your daughter and you might create something together. This could be any of the above suggestions, or something else that you enjoy doing together; such as, cross stitch or embroider favorite flowers or animals or sayings that indicate your family's beliefs about adult responsibilities. The handiwork can then be displayed in the house to remind your daughter of her connection to you and the family's values. Crocheting or knitting an afghan blanket which becomes a keepsake for her. Mastering a piano piece for four hands or a duet of any kind which is then performed for the family as your special shared acknowledgment of her passage out of childhood.

Ideas which include family and friends in the celebrations can be as simple or as elaborate as your daughter and family want to make them:

- The family makes a special cultural evening for the daughter by going out to a live performance of her choice. This could be folk dancing or ballet, theater, concert in the park, opera, or other musical theater. Make sure that somewhere during the evening's activities you allude to her transition and the family's acceptance of her as a more mature family member. This can be accomplished before or after the event with a simple spoken statement or a special card prepared by the family.

- Close family members might take a walk along a favorite river or around a lake. During the walk, family members can express their feelings about growing up, becoming an adult, learning to be responsible for their bodies in new ways. Respecting nature and nature's cycles are good topics which help guide the conversations about the cyclic aspect of menstruation.

- Have a picnic in her favorite park with her favorite foods and dessert. Prepare a daisy chain, ivy garland, or ring of flowers for her to wear on her head to show her revered status for the day. In between playing games, preparing, setting out, and cleaning up the food, have family and friends take her for walks to tell her something special that they admire about her and which they hope she maintains into her adulthood.

- Organize a potluck party for family, relatives, and friends. Everyone, including your daughter, divides into small troupes to present skits using fairy tales which have been modified to reflect positive female role-models, improvising, often to fit this special occasion.

- Gather as many present and past menstruating women family members as possible on the night of the first full moon after the girl has reached menarche (or any other time you and your daughter choose). Ask each woman to tell a story about a female family member who was influential in her adult life and why. The group can share tea and sweets, or other treats.

Think about this first celebration as beginning a tradition for your family and use the structure for each daughter or niece as she reaches menarche. Add a special touch specific for each girl's taste, interest, or personality. The celebration, whether simple or elaborate, becomes an important acknowledgment for your daughter or special girl and adds richness to her personal story of menstruation.

Final Thoughts

By your excitement, enthusiasm, and determination to teach your daughter about menstruation and to celebrate it with her, you allow your daughter to have positive experiences associated with this extraordinary time of life. After all, you and your daughter deserve to look back on her beginning journey into womanhood with fond memories.

Advanced Explanation of Menstruation

Many girls have irregular cycles in the early years. Whether a girl's cycle is regular or irregular, her body goes through a series of hormonal changes which trigger the events of menstruation. The hormones of the menstrual cycle regulate one another through a negative feedback system. This means that one hormone stimulates the increase or decrease of another hormone depending on the levels of each hormone in the bloodstream. Each time I review these phases, I am always amazed at the intricate and delicate balance of female hormones.

Menstruation is divided into four phases. The first phase is the Menstrual Phase (Days 1–5) which begins if the ovum is not fertilized. Menstrual flow begins when the uterine lining (endometrium) is shed due to low levels of estrogen in the blood. The low level of estrogen also stimulates the hypothalamus to release Gonadotrophin Releasing Hormone (GnRH). GnRH in turn stimulates the pituitary gland to release Follicle Stimulating Hormone (FSH).

The second phase is called the Follicular Phase (Day 6–12). FSH flows through the bloodstream to the ovaries where it triggers the maturation of several follicles and their ova in the ovaries. The developing follicles produce estrogen. Follicular phase ends as estrogen increases and signals the hypothalamus and pituitary gland to reduce FSH and begin secreting luteinizing (Lu-ton-i-zing) hormone (LH).

The third phase is called the Ovulatory Phase (Day 13–15). The surge of luteinizing hormone (LH) stops the growth of all ova except one. This ovum is released from the ovary and begins its journey in the oviduct. At birth a girl has approximately 400,00 ova (eggs) in each ovary. It is estimated that between 300 to 500 ova will develop or mature throughout a woman's reproductive live.

The fourth phase is called the Premenstrual Phase (Day 16–28).   This phase is divided into two parts. The first, the Luteal Phase (Day 16-23), begins when the empty follicle evolves into the corpus luteum (COR-pus LU-teum) which means "yellow body." Corpus luteum secretes progesterone into the bloodstream. Progesterone increases the uterine lining. If the ovum is fertilized by a sperm, then the corpus luteum continues to produce progesterone. If the ovum is not fertilized, estrogen and progesterone production tapers off. The low level of progesterone signals the pituitary gland to stop production of LH.

During Part 2 of the Premenstrual Phase (Day 24–28), the low levels of estrogen and progesterone stimulate the hypothalamus to release GnRH. This starts the menstrual cycle once again for without progesterone the uterine lining begins to break down. Day 1 of the Menstrual Phase is the first day of menstrual bleeding.

Many girls have irregular cycles in the early years. It is easy to understand why this happens. In fact in the early months after menarche many girls do not ovulate. They may skip of month or two. It takes a while for the body to regulate the hormone production.

Menstrual Difficulties

Painful periods are thought to be caused by hormonal changes. The technical term is dysmenorrhea (dis-MEN-or-rea-a). Infrequent periods are thought to be a result of abnormalities of the hypothalamus, pituitary gland, or ovaries. The medical term is oligomenorrhea (o-LE-go-men-or-he-a) and it is recommended that you consult your physician if your daughter has fewer than the usual 11 to 13 periods per year. Amenorrhea (A-men-or-re-a) means that the female started her period, but is not currently menstruating. The most common causes are: illness, weight loss, vigorous exercise, and stress. Once again, if you suspect that your daughter is no longer having her period, then it is advisable to consult your physician. Girls who become anorexic not only stop their periods, but can also suppress the growth of their internal sex organs. The opposite of slight or no periods, is heavy periods called menorrhagia (MEN-or-HA-gi-a). If the period lasts for more than 7 days, has especially large blood clots, or flooding occurs, call your physician. Heavy periods are usually caused by menstrual hormonal disturbances. There is, however, the possibility that heavy periods may be caused by fibroid tumors, or pelvic infections.

Glossary for Young Girls and their Parents

This Glossary is written to explain menstruation concepts in a manner understandable to young girls. Girls often comment that dictionaries offer little help with understanding menstrual terms. Here is an example from Webster's New Collegiate Dictionary:

> menstruation\men(t)-stre-wa-stra-\ n: a discharging of blood, secretions, and tissue debris from the uterus that recurs in nonpregnant breeding-age primate females at approximately monthly intervals and that is considered to represent a readjustment of the uterus to the nonpregnant state following proliferative changes accompanying the preceding ovulation; also period.

The girls are right! Dictionary descriptions of menstruation are usually completely meaningless to young girls.

Many girls are "grossed out" by these menstruation terms and anatomical names, and they wonder who dreamed up such words. In fact, parts of the body have strange names because they were described a long time ago by their physical appearance, not their function, since their functions were not known. Today the functions are known, but the old names still remain.

The words in this Glossary will be found in Webster's dictionary, but these definitions will not. As has been stated throughout this book, humor is a good thing during menstruation talks, and many of these definitions are lighthearted.

This Glossary may be used in a number of ways. First, it can serve as a resource for you when you want additional information to answer your daughter's questions. I hope that this Glossary will inspire your creativity. Your explanations are more meaningful and memorable for your daughter if you include your own experiences. Second, this section can function simply as a dictionary for your daughter's private use. And, third, it can be read as a section on its own, serving as a quick overview of terms which young girls often find confusing.

ACNE: Small sores that occur on and around the face, neck and back of girls and boys during adolescence. Also called pimples, bad complexion, and zits. There are two types of acne: blackheads and whiteheads.

Acne is no fun for the girl who has it. She may feel embarrassed and very sensitive. As someone who had terrible acne as a teenager, I (the author) remember the emotional pain quite well! There were times when I did not want to leave the house because of it. I thought people would think that I was unclean and did not wash well enough. It was only years later that I learned that acne has nothing to do with scrubbing one's face. Acne occurs because the oil glands under the skin produce excess oil which traps bacteria and clogs pores causing redness, swelling and irritation. Acne is a very common skin condition for adolescents.

As the adolescent growth spurt reaches its peak, hormone production is increased. It is generally thought that a hormonal imbalance causes acne, but a family history of acne, or an allergic reaction to foods or cosmetics can all influence whether or not a person has acne. As hormone levels increase in the blood, oil glands begin to secrete an oil called sebum. Sebum (se-bum) comes from sebaceous (se-bay-shus) glands which are found just under the skin near the pores. Large numbers of sebaceous glands are located on the face, neck, shoulder, chest, and back. This explains why individuals who have acne have the worst outbreaks on these areas.

Oil from sebaceous glands travels through pores and can cause oily looking skin. If the pores become clogged, a blackhead is likely to form. Blackheads are not caused by having dirty skin. Whiteheads are also caused by oil which becomes trapped under the skin. Instead of forming a blackhead, they form whitish bumps.

Sometimes acne can become severe and lead to cysts. Picking blackheads, whiteheads or cysts is not recommended and can result in permanent scarring. If acne persists or is painful, consult a dermatologist. There are medications which can help.

Acne usually disappears at the end of adolescence or early adulthood when oil glands produce less oil. Acne can reappear when people are under stress or have other situations which cause hormonal imbalances.

Having acne, however, is not a good reason to stay home and miss out on the fun. Years from now, no one will remember the acne but your daughter will remember if she missed an important dance or event.

ADOLESCENCE: The developmental stage between childhood and early adulthood when a child's body matures and changes into that of an adult. It is one of the longer stages of growth and development in children's lives. Adolescence begins at approximately 10 to 13 years of age for most girls, and 11 to 14 for most boys. It ends at approximately 17 to 18 years old for both.

Changes begin occurring unnoticed inside girls' bodies a few years before changes are noticed on the outside. At around eight years old, a girl's pituitary gland, a small pea-sized structure in the brain, sends out a message to release chemicals, called hormones. One of these hormones is called estrogen. It is released into the girl's bloodstream at night while she sleeps. Estrogen triggers a girl's reproductive organs to begin increasing in size and to begin maturing.

Physical changes that occur during adolescence include: growing taller and heavier, growing pubic and underarm hair, growing facial hair (for boys), and developing breasts and beginning to menstruate (for girls). These body changes lead to sexual maturity or the ability to become pregnant. Adolescence may also be called puberty.

AXILLARY HAIR: Underarm hair.

ANCILLARY HAIR: Hair that grows under arms, on legs, and, for boys, on their faces (beards). Ancillary hair usually begins to grow one to two years after pubic hair has sprouted. A few girls begin underarm hair growth before pubic hair growth. This is unusual, but not abnormal.

ANUS: Opening where bowel movements (also called feces) leave the body. Anus is the opening or hole at the end of the digestive tract.

It is not a sex organ; but because of its location, it is included in the drawing of external sex organs. The anus has nothing to do with menstruation or pregnancy. See drawing on page 145.

AREOLA: (ah-REE-oh-la) The darker circle of tissue encircling the nipple on the breast.

BIRTH CONTROL: These are ways to prevent pregnancy. There are methods for both females and males to use to prevent the egg and sperm from joining and implanting in the uterus. If the egg and sperm do not join and implant in the uterus, the female does not become pregnant.

BIRTH CONTROL PILLS: Pills taken orally (by mouth) every day to prevent pregnancy or to regulate menstruation and cramps. Contrary to popular belief, a female does have a menstrual period when taking birth control pills. Usually the flow is light and only lasts 3 to 5 days. Birth control pills also make periods very predictable. Birth control pills must be recommended and prescribed by a medical doctor and are used only after a girl has started her period.

BLEEDING: Common term used to describe menstrual flow during a female's period. Many girls describe their menstrual flow as light, medium, or heavy bleeding. Also see *Menstrual Flow.*

BLOATED: Feeling some females have right before or during their menstrual periods. Many feel as if they weigh more and their clothes may feel too tight. In some cases, females actually do gain a few pounds. This weight gain is usually only the water which the body is holding in its cells. After a few days, the body stops holding the water and it is urinated away. Weight returns to normal. This bloated feeling can be uncomfortable, but it does not necessarily mean that anything is wrong.

BODY ODOR: During adolescence, sweat glands begin to produce extra sweat, also called perspiration. Perspiration begins to have a different scent, more of an "adult" odor. Sometimes this sweat may smell more if it is trapped in underarm hair.

Unlike in many other places in the world, in the United States we have become quite worried about having noticeable body odor, and we even make jokes about it. Regular bathing and showering will wash away the sweat, trapped germs, and dirt which tends to cause the odor.

Another body odor that is often worried about is odor from the vagina. During adolescence, sweat glands in the vagina also increase their production. This may have a scent to it, but it is not offensive unless there is an infection. There are many advertisements which make us think that vaginal odor is bad. They recommend that we buy douches and scented or perfumed pads. Young girls should not use commercial douches or perfumed pads because they can cause irritation or itching in the vulva area.

BOOBS: Slang term used for female breasts. See *Breast Development* below.

BREAST DEVELOPMENT: This process begins for most girls between 9 and 14 years of age. Every girl's body begins to grow breasts only when it is ready. Nothing can speed up breast development or slow it down. It is the natural presence of a hormone called estrogen which begins breasts development. Female breast growth is commonly divided by medical professionals into 5 stages. Girls are usually ready for a bra by the time they reach Stage 3. Some girls, however, are ready to wear a bra during Stage 2. For most girls, reaching Stage 5 takes about 4 to 5 years from Stage 2 ("breast bud"). It is important to remember that every girl is different and some may mature faster or slower than other girls. There is no one right way to mature.

A little known fact is that a few boys experience temporary breast growth. This growth lasts about 12 to 18 months, and then the breasts return to normal size for boys. (Just thought you might be interested!)

Breast Development—Sexual Maturity Rating Scale

	STAGE 1 (SMR 1): Breasts during childhood are flat and only the nipple is raised a little.
	STAGE 2 (SMR 2): Called the Breast Bud Stage Between about 8 to 12 years of age, a small amount of fat tissue begins to form under nipples and aureole. Aureole are the darker skin around the nipple. Nipples now stick out a little and may be noticed.
	STAGE 3 (SMR 3): Breasts continue to grow and become rounded. Nipples and aureole may increase in size. At this stage, many girls feel more comfortable wearing a bra or undershirt.
	STAGE 4 (SMR 4): Not all girls go through this stage. In this stage, nipples and aureole form a separate little lump or bump. This makes them stick out above the rest of the breasts.
	STAGE 5 (SMR 5): The mature or grown-up breasts which occur during middle adolescence (about 12 to 16 years of age).

CERVIX: (SER-viks) The word, cervix, means "neck," and it is the neck of the uterus. It is only about 1 inch long, and it extends down into the vagina. Menstrual flow travels through the cervix into the vagina and then out through the vaginal opening. See drawing on page 55.

CLITORIS: (Kli-tuh-ris) The female external sex organ found toward the front of the vulva. It is covered by the "clitoral hood" where the two sides of labia minora join. The clitoris is very sensitive to touch. In fact, the clitoris is one of the most sensitive parts of a female's body. When it is rubbed or pressed, there can result feelings of warmth or excitement, or tension-releasing sensations. See drawing on page145.

CRAMPS: See *Menstrual Cramps*

"CURSE": This is an outdated derogatory term to describe menstruation. A long time ago, some women felt that having a period every month was a "curse" for being born female. Generations ago, people did not understand how a woman could bleed every month and not be sick, or how a woman could carry a baby inside her and give birth. Since people did not understand about menstruation and childbirth, there were many taboos (things that women should not do). For example, in some cultures menstruating women could not go into places of worship or into fields of growing plants for fear that something awful would happen, like the plants would die. Today we understand about menstruation and are not afraid of women who are menstruating. We know that menstruation is a natural, healthy, normal part of being female, and plants do not die from menstruating women.

DEPO PROVERA: A form of birth control. This is an injection that some girls and women get from their doctor every three months. It protects against pregnancy and also stops menstruation almost completely in most women.

DEPRESSION: Feeling sad, down, or blue and crying or wanting to cry more than usual. Many girls say they feel depressed or sad right before their periods. Nothing feels quite right when we are depressed. Some girls feel that their friends no longer like them, or that they are not smart, and that things will never get better. A few days after the period begins, most females feel better and can hardly remember that they felt so terrible just a few days earlier.

DISCHARGE: See *Vaginal Discharge*.

DRIPS OR DRIPPING: Words used to explain how the menstrual blood feels when it comes out of the vagina onto a sanitary napkin or pad. Some girls feel the dripping while other girls do not feel the dripping menstrual flow.

DOUCHES: Liquid used to rinse out the inside of the vagina. Water or water mixed with vinegar or baking soda are the most common liquids used to flush the inside of the vagina. There are also commercial douche mixes which can be bought at grocery or drug stores. It is not good to douche on a regular basis because the vagina is constantly being cleaned by the naturally occurring vaginal mucus (also called vaginal discharge), even during menstruation. Sometimes using douches can wash out the helpful bacteria which keep the body healthy. Douche only when recommended by your doctor. If you suddenly notice a different smelling discharge from your vagina, go to the doctor to have this checked. Do not good to douche before seeing the doctor.

EGG: See *Ovum*.

EJACULATION: Sperm and other fluids forced out of a male's erect penis by muscle contractions. Ejaculation most often occurs when males masturbate or have sexual intercourse. Young boys occasionally ejaculate during their sleep. This is called "wet dreams." No one is exactly certain why these occur.

EMBRYO: An ovum (egg cell) fertilized by a sperm cell which implants in the lining of the uterus and normally grows for 9 months into a baby. Embryo is the stage of growth for the first 3 months after fertilization or conception. After 3 months, the embryo is called a fetus until birth. The embryo is nourished and fed by the lining of the mother's uterus.

EMOTIONAL OR EMOTIONS: Feelings such as fear, hate, love, anger, grief, or joy are called emotions. Emotions can change from one to another very quickly during adolescence. Some people who study the human body believe that emotions change very quickly from joy to sorrow, from love to hate, because of hormones. Many of these hormones increase during adolescence and might explain why girls and boys sometimes act moody. These rapid mood changes from happy to sad to frustrated are called acting "emotionally unstable."

During adolescence, these emotional changes can be quite upsetting to both adolescents and parents. Girls may talk back or use harsh, hateful tones of voice which they never used before. Parents may become upset and yell back or use harsher tones with their daughters. This usually makes for hurt feelings and tears. Many times the emotional ups and downs get worse right before a girl begins her period for the first time. This is not a fun time for anyone, but everyone must manage to get through it. I am almost 50 years of age and my mother is over 70 years of age. My mother still remembers how awful I behaved right before I started my period for the first time. I must have been very emotional for my mother to remember after all these years! What is even more amazing is that I do not remember this at all! I remember only a few ups and downs. Mothers, if your parents are alive, you might want to check out what they remember about your emotions during adolescence.

ENDOMETRIUM: (en-doe-ME-tre-um) See *Uterine Lining*

ERECTION: The penis is made of special tissue that allows increased amounts of blood flow into it when the male is sexually excited. The blood causes the penis to enlarge, harden, and become erect. The erect penis is necessary for the ejaculation of sperm. This condition is called an erection. Some of the stories in this book talk about how girls can get pregnant after they begin to menstruate. In order for a girl or a woman to get pregnant, sperm from a male's erect penis must enter a female's vagina and swim to her ovum (or egg). Boys have erections from birth throughout their lives. The average age for boys to begin puberty is 11 to 14 years old. During puberty, a boy's body begins to produce sperm as during puberty a girl's body begins to ripen ova. Once sperm is produced, a boy is capable of impregnating a female.

ESTROGEN: (ES-tro-jen) Female hormone made in the ovaries. When it is secreted into the bloodstream, a girl's body starts to change into a woman's. Estrogen also regulates the menstrual cycle.

FALLOPIAN TUBES: Common name for the small tube-like structures on both sides of the uterus where the sperm and ovum (egg) normally connect, causing fertilization of the egg. The more current accepted term is oviducts. See *Oviducts.*

FERTILIZATION OR FERTILIZE: Fertilization occurs during sexual intercourse if a sperm cell from the male connects with an ovum cell from the female. This process is also called conception. The female becomes pregnant, and approximately 9 months after conception a baby is born. Females are fertile during ovulation, which is normally 14 days before the first day of menstrual flow.

FLUSHING OUT: An expression for the shedding of the lining of the uterus during menstrual flow. This is one of the many ways of saying menstrual flow or menstrual blood.

FOLLICLE: One of many small sacks or glands located in each ovary. The follicles hold the ovum. See drawing on page 55.

GENITALS: Another name for external sex organs, but can also refer to internal sex organs. External means that we can see these sex organs when we look at a naked body (for example, the clitoris or penis). Internal sex organs means they are inside our body and cannot be seen with the naked eye (for example, the ovaries or testes). See drawing below for external female sex organs and see page 55 for drawing of internal female sex organs.

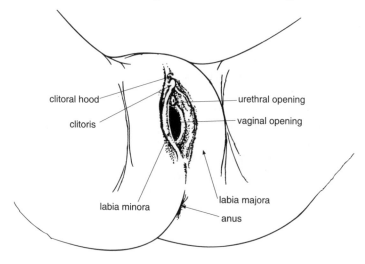

GROWTH SPURT: One major outward sign of adolescence is rapid growth and weight gain. It may begin as early as 8 to 9 years of age for some girls. Average peak of growth, however, is 12 years old. Boys have their growth spurt later in puberty than girls. The average age for boys is between 12 and 16.

During the growth spurt, girls may be taller and weigh more than boys. This can cause some girls and boys to feel uncomfortable around each other. Most girls reach their adult height by 14 or 15 years of age. Usually, girls grow taller first, and about 6 months later gain weight.

Girls also feel awkward or clumsy when their hands and feet grow larger before their arms and legs catch up. All this new body growth can cause many girls to feel self-conscious.

Leg and underarm hair grows and darkens as girls get older. This also causes some girls to feel self-conscious. Boys or other girls may tease them if their hair is noticeable. Parents need to help their daughter with the timing for shaving or hair removal, otherwise their daughter will be forced to solve this dilemma alone.

Boys sometimes tease girls about their changing bodies. Psychologists believe the reason that most people tease or make fun of other people is because they feel inferior. Boys who joke about girls' developing bodies are feeling insecure. They probably would not admit this, true as it is!

It is best to just ignore boys' irritating comments, although this is easier said than done. Parents need to talk with daughters about embarrassing and degrading comments which boys often make. Suggest that your daughter come to you for help in handling boys' or other girls' insulting remarks.

Parents may remember mean and hostile statements made during adolescence. They were probably said in jest, but hurt nonetheless because they struck vulnerable, tender spots. Try to relate your feelings of hurt and embarrassment when consoling your daughter who has had her sensitive, newly forming self-concept insulted and injured.

GYNECOLOGIST: A physician who sees only females for menstruation and other health care matters specific to females. It is recommended that girls see their family doctor or pediatrician for regular check-ups (which do not involve a pelvic exam). Usually, a gynecologist sees a girl either at age 18, if she is sexually active, or if she has a specific menstrual problem.

HEALTH HISTORY: Gynecologists and other physicians will ask questions about general health. Also, gynecologists usually want to know when the last menstrual period began. It is helpful to keep a record of when your period begins. You can mark your calendar the first day of your period and when you expect your next one. Then you can be prepared with sanitary pads or tampons.

HOMEOPATHIC DOCTOR: A doctor who relies on the natural substances found in many plants, rather than on other types of medicine, to treat specific medical conditions. Some women go to homeopathic doctors for help with menstrual cramps.

HORMONES: Chemicals made in glands and carried by the bloodstream to other parts of the body. During adolescence, some hormones made in the pituitary gland in the brain travel through the bloodstream and signal the body to grow and the sex organs to mature.

It is difficult to understand how hormones work. Hormones begin the adolescent growth stage without anyone knowing exactly when it starts. It is only after the hormones have started changing the body that we know adolescence has begun.

Two important hormones for female development are estrogen and progesterone.

HYMEN: The very thin layer of tissue, called a "membrane," that partially covers the opening to the vagina. It is difficult to see the hymen because it is inside the opening of the vagina. It can be broken or torn by many activities, like riding a horse or bicycle, doing the splits, or having sexual intercourse for the first time. A female can still be considered a virgin, even if her hymen has been broken. Years ago, people thought a sign of virginity was having an unbroken hymen that might bleed during the first intercourse. A few of the stories tell about mothers who did not want their daughters to use tampons because the hymen might be broken. Today we know that when the hymen breaks, there is no pain and very little blood, and that most females do not know when it breaks.

INNER WALLS: See *Uterine Lining*.

KOTEX: First widely used brand of sanitary napkins (pads). Kotex was introduced in the 1920s and is still used today. Many people called any sanitary napkins Kotex.

LABIA MAJORA: (LAY-bee-a mah-JORE-ah) "Labia" in Latin means "lips," and majora means "larger" or "bigger." These are the two outer larger folds of skin (big lips) on both sides of the vaginal opening. They are part of the female's external genitals.

During middle adolescence, when a girl is approximately 12- to 14-years-old, pubic hair begins to grow on the labia majora. The underneath side does not grow pubic hair and is basically smooth with some raised bumps. These bumps are oil glands. Oil gland secretions help to keep this area clean, moist, and free from irritation.

When we wipe ourselves after urination, we are wiping between the labia majora and labia minora (See Labia Minora). To insert a tampon, the labia majora and minora must be slightly spread apart in order to find the opening to the vagina. See drawing on page 145.

LABIA MINORA: (LAY-bee-a Mih-NORE-ah) These are located just underneath the labia majora. The words mean "small lips." They have the same function as labia majora. These two inner folds of skin which are smaller than the outer folds (labia majora) are found on both sides of the vaginal opening. They are a part of the vulva and part of the female external genitals. These folds of skin cover and protect the openings to the inside of the body. Labia minora do not grow pubic hair. See drawing on page 145.

LIPS: Common or slang name used for the labia majora and labia minora. See drawing on page 145.

LINING: See *Uterine Lining.*

MAXI PADS: Style of sanitary napkins which are worn on heavy flow days. Maxi pads are thick in order to absorb the heaviest menstrual flow. Many girls wear maxi pads at night while they sleep because they absorb more flow for a longer time. There are many different brands of maxi pads. Some of the stories in this book tell funny experiences about wearing large pads for the first few times.

MENARCHE: (MEN-ar-kee) A girl's very first period or menstrual flow is called menarche. After the first menstrual flow, all the others are called, simply, menstruation. After menarche, it is said that a female has started to menstruate. Some girls have their menarche as young as 8 years or as old as 15 years of age. Average age among girls in the United States is 12.

It can be both entertaining and educational to talk about how old other family members were when they first started menstruation. Studies show that if a girl's mother or sisters started early compared to their friends, then it is likely that the girl will start her period before she is 12 years old. This is only a guideline, but it will give an idea of when to expect and prepare for menarche. It makes no difference when you start—you're still "normal."

MENSES: Another term for menstrual or blood flow from the uterus. This word is not often used in conversations, but it does appear in textbooks. Health books and physicians may use menses instead of menstrual flow.

MENOPAUSE: The end of a woman's menstruation, and the end of her ability to have children. Hormone changes within older women begin menopause just as hormone changes within young girls begin menstruation. Menopause usually begins when women are about 50 years old. As is true with menstruation, some women go through menopause earlier and some later. When women no longer ovulate, they do not have a monthly period and cannot become pregnant. Some women look forward to menopause because they have had their children and no longer want to menstruate. Some women are not ready for menopause and miss having a monthly period. Menopause takes a number of years to complete. In some instances, mothers may be going through menopause about the same time that their daughters are beginning to menstruate. This means that hormonal changes can be the cause of many emotional ups and downs for both mother and daughter.

MENSTRUAL BLOOD: Menstrual flow is made up of blood, tissue from the endometrial lining, the egg and other body fluids. It can look either bright red, dark red or brown. The blood makes the menstrual flow look red; the other things make it look dark. It looks like there is more blood than there actually is in the menstrual flow.

MENSTRUAL CYCLE: The regular phases which occur in the uterus and sex organs connected with menstruation. There are 4 phases of the cycle: Phase 1: Menstruation begins with the uterus bleeding or shedding its lining. Menstruation lasts about 3 to 7 days. Phase 2: Preovulation. The lining of the uterus builds up. An ovum matures in the ovary (sac). Phase 3: Ovulation. The ripened ovum leaves the ovary and starts its journey down the oviduct. Phase 4: Premenstruation. The uterine lining continues to thicken and the ovum continues its journey. If the ovum is not fertilized by a sperm cell, the body gets ready to shed or lose the uterus lining and the unfertilized ovum.

The whole cycle usually take 28 to 30 days and then begins again. The body makes new tissue to replace what was lost during menstruation. These 4 phases continue monthly as long as the female is menstruating. See diagram on pages 56-57.

MENSTRUAL CRAMPS: Muscle contractions in the uterus during menstrual flow (period). There may also be cramps or pain in the lower back during periods. Some girls have no cramps or pain, other girls have cramps during some periods, and some girls have cramps almost every time they have a period. Menstrual cramps can be relieved by using a heating pad, over-the counter pain medicine, or raspberry leaf tea. If cramps are disrupting to a girl's normal routine it is important that she see her family doctor, a gynecologist or a pediatrician. Physicians can prescribe pain relievers for menstrual cramps.

MENSTRUAL FLOW: Term to describe the blood, body tissue, and fluids, plus an unfertilized egg, that flows out of the uterus. The amount of blood that comes out varies. Some females have almost no loss of blood while others have more. Menstrual flow is called light, medium, or heavy depending on how much flow there is and how many days it lasts. Most females flow (or menstruate) for about 4 to 5 days, and during that time may lose from 1 to 16 tablespoons of blood. Menstrual flow is also called menstruation, period, or menstrual blood.

MENSTRUATION: The natural, healthy monthly flow of a bloody fluid from the uterus during a woman's life from puberty to menopause. The fluid (menstrual blood or flow) is made of tissues from the lining of the uterus, mucus and blood. The fluid can have a dark brown to red color. It usually does not clot, but flows slowly from the uterus. Monthly menstruation is brought about by a reduction of the hormone, progesterone, in the bloodstream. Reduction of progesterone occurs when the ovum (egg) is not fertilized. The monthly process of menstrual flow is the time when the uterus cleans itself.

Girls usually begin to menstruate for the first time around 12 years old. Menstruation occurs on average every 28 to 30 days. The cycle can vary from 18 to 40 days.

A woman does not menstruate when she is pregnant. She may not menstruate regularly if she is ill, very nervous, has not eaten properly, or is vigorously training as an athlete. If a girl begins to menstruate and then menstruates irregularly or stops menstruating altogether, it is best to consult a doctor.

MIGRAINE HEADACHE: A very painful headache with sharp pains around the forehead. These can occur during or prior to menstruation. Sometimes the person feels sick to her stomach and vomits. Sunlight, light from light bulbs, and noise may make her migraine headache worse. Migraine headache sufferers need to consult with a doctor for help with the pain.

MINI PADS: Sanitary napkins which are worn on light flow days. Mini pads are thin and absorb less fluid than maxi pads. There are many different brands available at grocery and drug stores. Some girls wear maxi pads on days when their menstrual flow is heavy, and mini pads on days when their menstrual flow is lighter. Many of the stories in this book talk about the differences in sanitary napkins.

MODESS: Brand name of a popular sanitary napkin. In some of the stories in this book, the women refer to a sanitary napkin or pad by the brand name, Modess or Kotex. Modess and Kotex were the two leading brands of sanitary napkins from 1920 through the 1970's. Today there are many different names and brands, so we normally hear girls call sanitary napkins either maxi or mini pads.

MONS: Its longer name is "mons pubis" (monz-PEW-bis). It is fatty tissue covering the pubic bones. Pubic hair grows on the mons pubis during puberty. Mons also provides a protective covering over the pubic bones.

MONTHLY CYCLE: Another name for menstrual cycle.

MUCOUS: See *Vaginal Discharge.*

NEST: Used to describe the inside of the uterus as it prepares to receive a fertilized ovum. Also see *Uterine Lining.*

O.B.'s: Brand name of tampons. They come in different sizes—mini, regular, and super. Also see *Tampons.*

"ON THE RAG": A slang expression that means menstruating. Years ago females used cloth rags to catch menstrual flow so it did not stain their clothes. Rags were washed so that they could be used again. Rags were used before there were sanitary napkins and tampons. Some women today are returning to cloth pads for ecological reasons. Women used to say that they were "on the rag" to mean that it was their period or menstruation.

Today, "on the rag" is a saying that has acquired negative meaning. People often say someone is "on the rag" when they think that the person is acting in a way they do not like. Sometimes when a girl is crying, upset, or angry, someone (usually a boy who doesn't even know what it means) will say that the girl is "on the rag." In this instance, menstruation is being blamed for the girl's behavior, even if she is not menstruating.

OVA: Plural for ovum. Means more than one egg or ovum. Also see *Ovum.*

OVARIES: Two small almond-shaped glands or sacs, one on each side of the uterus, which hold the egg cells (ova). Each ovary is attached to the uterus with a ligament to hold it in correct relationship to the oviducts. Ovaries also produce female hormones which help a girl's body grow into a mature woman's body of breasts, hips, and waist. See drawing on page 55.

OVIDUCTS: Two thin, delicate structures connected to the top of the uterus with one oviduct on each side of the uterus. One end of each oviduct is connected to the uterus, while the other end is free to slowly move about in a small swinging motion. Each free end sweeps over one ovary to pick up an ovum (egg) when it matures and ruptures out of the ovary. When the ovum jumps out of the ovary, it is called ovulation. Each time a female ovulates, the ovum travels down the oviduct to the uterus. See drawing on page 55. Also see *Ovulation.*

OVULATION: Time of the month when an ovum (egg) is released from one of the ovaries. The ovum or egg is caught by one of the two oviducts and begins its journey down to the uterus. It is during this time that females are fertile and able to become pregnant if sperm connects with the ovum.

It is difficult for most females to know exactly when they ovulate. One way to know (even though it is after the fact) is to count backwards 14 days from the first day of the period. Females almost always ovulate and then exactly 14 days later begin to menstruate. Most books and pamphlets say that females will ovulate on or around day 14 of their menstrual cycle. This is true if the female has a 28 day menstrual cycle—ovulation would be on day 14 counting backwards from 28. It is the last 14 days of the cycle, however, that predict ovulation and signal menstruation, not the first 14 days.

What if a female's cycle is longer or shorter than 28 days? For example, if a female normally has a 32-day cycle, then approximately 18 days into her cycle would be her ovulation day. She would then begin her period 14 days later on day 32. In addition, if a female is sick, excited, sad, stressed, overly tired, dieting, or in a strenuous workout program, ovulation may come earlier or later than normal. One can understand why predicting ovulation and menstruation has been difficult for most females. A female is fertile and can become pregnant immediately before, during, or 2 to 3 days after ovulation.

OVUM (EGG): Many people call the ovum an egg. The ovum is a tiny reproductive cell stored in the ovaries. An ovum is very small and can only be seen with a microscope. The plural of ovum is ova. All the ova a female will have are present at birth in her ovaries. At puberty, the first ovum begins to mature and one ovum matures for each menstrual cycle until menopause. There are approximately 400,000 ova in each ovary.

Usually only one ovum is released each month into a oviduct. This process is called ovulation. During ovulation if two ova are released and sperm connects with them, then twins could be born. These would be fraternal twins and would be no more alike than other brothers and sisters. If only one ovum is in the oviduct and connects with sperm and that one fertilized ovum divides, then identical twins could be born. The twins will be either both girls or both boys and look like each other.

PADS: Another more common name for sanitary pads or napkins. Also see *Sanitary Pads*.

PAIN RELIEVERS: Medicines to help stop or reduce menstrual cramps and back pain which can be bought either with or without a prescription. In some of the stories in this book, the girls and women tell when they had cramps and did not go to the pharmacy or doctor for help. They all recommend that females go for help.

PANTYLINERS: Very thin absorbent pads that fit in the crotch of the underpants and stick to them. These can be used as sanitary napkins for very light flow days. Some females wear these for vaginal discharge on days between their period. Many girls begin wearing these 1 or 2 days before they start their periods each month to keep from staining their clothes and being embarrassed if they start flowing in public.

PELVIS: The bones around your hips. These bones form a basin-like container. The female internal sex organs are inside this boney basin.

PENIS: The male sex organ used both for urinating and (when erect) for releasing sperm. Sperm is released from the penis during orgasm. Orgasms can occur during masturbation, nocturnal emission, and sexual intercourse. The muscles in the penis contract during orgasm and push a white-milky liquid with sperm out the end of the penis.

PERIOD: Another word for menstruation. "Period" is the most common word used to talk about the time (usually 5 -7 days) when a female is having her menstrual flow. Other expressions for menstruating are: "girl trouble," "that time of the month," "my friend is visiting," or "my red-headed cousin is here." Also see *Menstrual Flow.*

PERSPIRATION: This is a more formal word for sweat. Perspiration begins to have an odor around adolescence. It is important to bathe regularly to reduce your chances of body odor from perspiration. Many countries of the world do not mind body odor; in fact, some peoples of the world like the smell of body odor. This, however, is not true for the United States. Adolescents tell cruel jokes and even make fun of people with body odor.

PIMPLES: Another word for acne. These are small sores that form on the face and back. They can fill with pus because of infection in the pores of the skin. Most everyone has the urge to pop their pimples. It is best not to pop pimples because this can cause the skin to have a permanent scar. Pimples may be a signal that adolescence is fast approaching. Just as hormonal changes in the body cause breasts and pubic hair to grow, they also increase production of the oil glands in the skin, causing pimples. Blocked pores are called blackheads. Blackheads happen when the oil is exposed to air. A blackhead does not mean that your face is dirty. Also see *Acne*

PLAYTEX: Another brand name of sanitary pads and tampons.

PREMENSTRUAL SYNDROME (PMS): One or two weeks before the monthly menstrual flow (period), some females feel moody, cry or get mad easier than other times of the month. Some girls and women may also experience weight gain, head and backaches, and breast tenderness right before their periods. PMS can also include cravings for salty and sugary foods. After the period begins, PMS symptoms go away.

Some females never have PMS symptoms, others have them occasionally, and still others have PMS symptoms almost every month. If a female has PMS or thinks that she does, she can go to her physician for help. Suggestions normally include: (1) exercising regularly, (2) reducing or not eating or drinking foods with caffeine (colas, chocolate, etc.), and (3) eating regularly. Some doctors may recommend vitamins also. It is best to see a physician for specific problems. However, these recommendations are always good ones to follow for a healthy body.

PUBERTY: The time during adolescence, usually between 10 and 17 years old, when a child reaches sexual maturity. Also see *Adolescence*.

PUBIC HAIR: Hair that grows around sexual organs of females and males during puberty. Pubic hair is usually coarser and can be curlier than hair on one's head. For some girls, growing pubic hair is exciting, and they like to watch for new growth. For other girls, growing pubic hair is no big deal. Whichever is true, pubic hair grows in its own time and its own way.

Pubic Hair Development—Sexual Maturity Rating Scale

	STAGE 1 (SMR 1): Preadolescents have no pubic hair present on vulva.
	STAGE 2 (SMR 2): Sparse, slightly pigmented, downy hair, usually straight or only somewhat curled. Grows along sides of labia majora.
	STAGE 3 (SMR 3): Hair becomes darker, coarser, more curled, begins to grow on mons.
	STAGE 4 (SMR 4): Looks similar to adult pubic hair as it becomes darker, coarser, grows in a triangular shape, but does not cover as much of the mons as in adult.
	STAGE 5 (SMR 5): Increased quantity, covers mons, and has reached adult growth. (See Sexual Maturity Rating of Pubic Hair.)

SANITARY NAPKINS: Another word for Sanitary Pads. See below.

SANITARY PADS: Thin absorbent pads that are put in the crotch of the underpants and held there by adhesive strips. Adhesive strips are placed inside the underpants and keep the pad from moving. Sanitary napkins used to be held in place by a belt or pins. Some stories in this book tell about these and how they were uncomfortable to wear. See also Sanitary Belts.

There are many different kinds of pads. Most are made of absorbent material that is light weight. Pads come in different sizes from maxi, sometimes called super, (for heavier flow days) to regular and mini (for lighter flow days). Pads also come in different shapes. Many girls try different shapes and sizes to see which feels best for them. It is best to not use deodorant pads. Pads with built in deodorant can irritate the vulva.

SANITARY BELT: Before pads with adhesive strips became available, there were only big bulky pads with a tail on each end for females to wear to catch their menstrual flow. The tails had to be inserted into an elastic belt which was worn around the waist. The belt had 2 little hooks which hung down and held the pad between the legs. The front tail came up to the belt near the belly button. In back, the tail came up between the buttock and hooked on the belt. This was still not very comfortable, but when compared to the rags that were either just placed or safety-pinned in underpants, the belt was a great invention. Today belts and safety pins are still available, but most girls and women use the new adhesive strip pads that stick to the underwear.

SEX ORGANS: See drawings of female internal and external sex organs on pages 55 and 145.

SEXUAL MATURITY: When a girl is capable of reproducing and having children.

SEXUAL REPRODUCTION: Process of getting pregnant and giving birth to children. Reproductive life for a female is the time between her first period (menarche) and her last one (menopause). Once a young girl reaches puberty, many families begin to treat her differently. Some families will treat her as more of an adult because she can now become pregnant. Other families will be uncomfortable with the girl's bodily changes and ability to have babies. Being capable of reproducing or conceiving babies is a normal part of physical development. Parents and children need to be able to talk to each other about the decisions involving sexual activity which could result in reproduction.

SHED: This word is used to explain menstrual flow or bleeding. The flow begins when the lining inside the uterus is shed or flows out of the body through the vagina. Sometimes doctors will use this word to describe the process of menstruation.

SPERM: The reproductive cells made by males who have gone through puberty. Sperm is made in the male's testicles. Boys are able to produce sperm around age 14.

TAMPONS: A tube-shaped roll of absorbent, cotton-like material with a string attached to one end. The tampon is manually inserted into the vagina to catch menstrual flow before it comes out of the vaginal opening.

Tampons come in regular and super sizes for lighter or heavier flow. Most plumbing can handle tampons, and you can flush them down the toilet. However, tampons can clog old plumbing. To be on the safe side, wrap tampons in toilet paper and throw them in the trash.

Girls may wonder if the tampon will get lost inside the vagina or if the tampon will get stuck. The answer is "no." Tampons fit into the vagina and go no farther. A tampon is too big to fit through the cervix into the uterus. To remove a tampon, simply pull the string down and out comes the tampon. You will read stories in this book of girls who thought their tampons were stuck. They are harder to get out when the vagina is dry, but they do come out.

Many people have been told that tampons are not good for girls, and that girls should wait to use them until after they are married or have a baby. Today we know that there is no medical reason for a girl to wait until she is married. Some religions and cultures caution females not to use tampons because use of a tampon could break the hymen. These beliefs will dictate whether females will use tampons.

Some females do not use tampons at all. However, many girls and women use only tampons. Others use a combination of pads and tampons depending on their flow and how often they can conveniently change them.

Some tampons have cardboard or plastic applicators to make them easier to insert into the vagina. Some girls prefer the tampons with applicators while others like tampons without applicators. Either way, tampons must be inserted into the vagina using your fingers to help guide the way.

Those who are more ecologically minded may want to try the tampons without applicators, because there is less cardboard or plastic to throw away. If you decide to use tampons, experiment with a variety of brands and sizes. Some brands will be more comfortable than others.

TAMPAX OR PLAYTEX OR OB'S: Three brand names of tampons. OB's are a little different from Tampax or Playtex. OB's do not have an applicator and you use your finger to open your labia. They are a little harder to insert, but are small and have no outside plastic or cardboard to throw away afterwards.

TESTICLES: Sex organs in a male's scrotum which produce sperm. Males normally have two testicles. Each testicle is held outside the male's body in the scrotum. The scrotum hangs down a little behind the penis.

TISSUES: Group of thin layers of cells connected together. Skin, for instance, is made of tissues. The inside lining of the uterus is made of tissues, some of which come off during menstruation.

TOXIC SHOCK SYNDROME (TSS): A serious illness thought to be caused by a bacterium infection. One possible cause of TSS is failure to change tampons frequently enough. It is rare that a girl would have Toxic Shock Syndrome, but it can be serious enough to result in death. There are about 50 to 100 cases of TSS reported in the United States each year. About half of the reported cases are related to menstruation, the other half result from nonvaginal wounds and abrasions. One case was even caused by a dirty tattoo needle.

Some of the signs of TSS are: high fever (usually over 102 degrees), diarrhea, vomiting, and a reddish rash like a sunburn. The rash is usually found on the stomach, back, and neck, but can also be found on hands and feet. After a while the rash begins to peel. It is easiest to see the peeling on the palms of the hands and on the feet.

If anyone has any of these signs while wearing a tampon, REMOVE IT IMMEDIATELY AND ASK FOR HELP. Instruct girls to go for help. IF AT SCHOOL, TELL TEACHERS, SCHOOL NURSES, OR P.E. TEACHERS. IF AT HOME, TELL YOUR PARENTS, OR ANY PERSON WHO CAN HELP YOU. IF NO ONE IS AROUND, THEN CALL YOUR DOCTOR AND EXPLAIN TO THE NURSE HOW YOU ARE FEELING AND THAT YOU HAD BEEN WEARING A TAMPON. Even though this disease is rare, it can make a person very sick, very quickly. If no one can be reached to help, then call "911" or a hospital emergency room and talk to a nurse on duty. If untreated, this disease will not go away, and may cause death.

UTERUS: The pear-shaped sex organ inside females which expands as a baby grows inside it. The uterus is located in the middle of the lower abdominal area and is made of muscles. The uterus is hollow and compact when a baby is not growing inside of it. Also called a womb. See drawing on page 55.

UTERINE LINING: Also known as endometrium or Inner Walls, it is the mucous membrane lining the inner surface of the uterus. Endometrial lining builds up every month in order to nourish a fertilized ovum. If the ovum is not fertilized, the endometrial lining is shed as menstrual flow. When an ovum is fertilized, it implants in the endometrial lining, and a baby grows. See drawing on page 55.

VAGINA: An internal sex organ in females. It opens at the top to the uterus, and its bottom opening is at the vulva. Menstrual blood flows from the uterus through the vagina out through the vulva.

Think of the vagina as a cloth purse made of soft velvet. When there is nothing in the purse, it is flat; but, when you place things inside, it expands or gets bigger. This is true for your vagina. It will expand when a tampon is placed inside it. The vagina also expands during childbirth for the child to come from the uterus through the vagina and into the world.

The vagina is very important for a female's overall health because it serves as a barrier to germs which could harm other female organs. See drawing on page 55.

VAGINAL DISCHARGE: These are big words which simply mean that a small amount of milky white or clear water-like liquid comes from your vagina. This is completely normal. Vaginas begin to make this mucus-liquid right before a girl's period for the first time and prior to all the other periods.

This discharge is mostly mucus. It is similar to mucus in the nose. A runny nose or watering eyes help to wash out germs the same way as vaginal mucus (called discharge) does. When this mucus dries on underpants, it may leave a yellowish stain.

Females also have a vaginal discharge when they have a vaginal infection. This discharge will often have a strong odor that will signal the difference between normal discharge and infection. If there is a different, stronger odor, call a physician.

VIRGIN OR VIRGINITY: A person who has not yet had sexual intercourse is called a virgin. The time in a girl or boy's life prior to their first sexual intercourse is called their virginity.

VULVA: The part of female sex organs that are on the outside of the body (also called external genitals). Vulva is made up of labia majora and minora, clitoris, urinary and vaginal openings, and anus. The only way to see the vulva is to use a mirror. Hold it between the legs, and separate the labia majora (outer) folds of skin. Drawings of vulvas look different than real ones. No one's vulva looks exactly like the drawing. See drawing on page 145.

WOMB: See *Uterus.*

Suggested Reading

For Mothers

Apter, Terri (1990). *Altered Loves*. New York: Fawcett-Columbine

Bailey, Susan (1992). *How Schools Shortchange Girls*. Sponsored by American Association of University Women

Brown, Lyn Mikel, and Carol Gilligan (1992). *Meeting at the Crossroads*. Cambridge, MA: Harvard University Press

Brumberg, Joan Jacobs (1997). *The Body Project: An Intimate History of American Girls*. New York: Random House

Debold, Elizabeth, Wilson, Marie, Malave, Idelisse (1993). *From Betrayal to Power: Mother Daughter Revolution*. Reading, MA: Addison-Wesley Publishing Company

Delaney, Janice, Lupton, Mary Jane, and Toth, Emily (1988). *The Curse: A Cultural History of Menstruation*. Urbana, IL: University of Illinois Press

Eder, Donna (1995). *School Talk: Gender and Adolescent Culture*. New Brunswick, NJ: Rutgers University Press

Gilligan, Carol (1982). *In A Different Voice*. Cambridge, MA: Harvard University Press

Hancok, Emily (1989). *The Girl Within*. New York: Fawcett Books

Jordan, Judith, Kaplan, Alexandra, Miller, Jean Baker, Stiver, Irene, and Surrey, Janet 1991). *Women's Growth In Connection*. New York: Guilford Press

Kerr, Barbara (1985). *Smart Girls, Gifted Women*. Columbus, OH: Ohio Psychology Publishing

Pipher, Mary (1994). *Reviving Ophelia, Saving the Selves of Adolescent Girls*. New York: Ballantine Books

Pipher, Mary (1996) *The Shelter of Each Other, Rebuilding Our Families*. New York: Grosset/Putnam Book

Steinem, Gloria (1983). *Outrageous Acts and Everyday Rebellions*. New York: New American Library (especially the sessay "If Men Could Menstruate.")

Stein, Nan, Marshall, Nancy, and Tropp, Linda (1993). *Secrets in Public Sexual Harassment in Our Schools*. Cosponsored by NOW Legal Defense and Education Fund and Wellesley College Center for Research onWomen

Taylor, Dena (1988). *Red Flower: Rethinking Menstruation*. Freedom, CA: The Crossing Press

For Mothers and Daughters

Blume, Judy (1970). *Are You There God? It's Me, Margaret*. New York: Dell Publishing

Gardner-Loulan, JoAnn, Lopez, Bonnie, and Quackenbush, Marcia (1991). *Period*. Volcano, CA: Volcano Press

Gravelle, Karen and Gravelle, Jennifer (1996). *The Period Book: Everything You Don't Want To Ask (But Need To Know)*. New York: Walker and Company

Harris, Robie (1994). *Changing Bodies, Growing Up, Sex & Sexual Health: It's Perfectly Normal*. Cambridge, MA: Candlewick Press

Hoch, Dean, and Hoch, Nancy (1990). *The Sex Education Dictionary for Today's Teens & Pre-Teens*. Pocatello, ID: Landmark Publishing

Madaras, Lynda (1988). *The What's Happening to My Body? Book for Girls*. New York: New Market Press

McCoy, Kathy and Wibbelsman, Charles (1992). *The New Teenage Body Book*. New York: The Body Press/Perigee Books

Index

More from Perspective Publishing

Perspective Publishing is a small independent publishing company which helps parents with the problems you face every day: discipline, friendship problems, talking with your kids, balancing work and family, challenging and inspiring your kids.

AMERICA'S DAUGHTERS: 400 Years of American Women
by Judith Head

This easy-to-read yet carefully researched history of American women from the 1600s to today is illustrated with 150 photos and period drawings, and gives children and adults both an overview of what life was like for women, and profiles of more than 50 individual women, both famous and not so well known.

ISBN: 0-9622036-8-8 Paperback. 8"x10"; 128 pages; $16.95

Win the Whining War & Other Skirmishes: A family peace plan
by Cynthia Whitham, MSW

This easy-to-use guide helps parents increase cooperation and reduce conflict with children ages 2-12. Step-by-step, parents learn how to cut out all the annoying behavior (tantrums, teasing, dawdling, interrupting, complaining, etc.) that drives them crazy.

ISBN: 0-9622036-3-7, paperback. 6"x9"; 208 pages; $13.95

"The Answer is NO": Saying it and sticking to it
by Cynthia Whitham, MSW

Tackling twenty-six situations that plague parents of 2 to 12-year-olds, this book helps parents define their values, build good parenting habits, and set firm, fair limits. Bedtime, pets, makeup, music, TV, homework, and designer clothes are just a few of the problems covered.

ISBN: 0-9622036-4-5, paperback. 6"x9"; 224 pages; $13.95l

Survival Tips for Working Moms: 297 REAL Tips from REAL Moms
by Linda Goodman Pillsbury

Full of examples of how the tips actually work in real families, this is a light but no-nonsense practical resource thast can help every working mom. From chores to childcare, errands to exercise, this book makes life easier. Almost 100 cartoons make this a book you can't put down.

ISBN: 0-9622036-5-3, paperback. 6"x9"; 192 pages; $10.95

Good Friends Are Hard to Find: Help your child find, make and keep friends
by Fred Frankel, Ph.D.

Step-by-step, parents learn to help their 5 to 12-year-olds make friends and solve problems with other kids. This guide also offers concrete help for teasing, bullying and meanness, both for the child who is picked on and for the tormentor. Based on UCLA's world renowned Children's Social Skills Program, this book teaches clinically tested techniques that really work.

ISBN: 0-9622036-7-X, paperback. 6"x9"; 242 pages; $13.95

Order now: 1-800-330-5851 or www.familyhelp.com

More from Perspective Publishing

Before She Gets Her Period: Talking to your daughter about menstruation
by Jessica B. Gillooly, Ph.D.

This friendly book has up-to-date information and uses real personal stories, exercises and activities to help parents talk with their daughters about menstruation — even if their daughters don't want to talk. It's the only book about menstruation written for parents.

ISBN: 0-9622036-9-6, paperback. 6"x9"; 166 pages; $13.95

The Invasion of Planet Wampetter
by Samuel H. Pillsbury
illustrated by Matthew Angorn

Pudgy orange young wampetters Eloise and Gartrude Tub save their planet from becoming an intergalactic tourist trap in this non-violent and funny space adventure. As entertaining for grown-ups as for kids, it is a perfect family read aloud.

ISBN: 0-9622036-6-1, hardcover. 6"x9"; 144 pages; $15.00

9 TO 5 IS THE EASY PART

MomShirts

9 TO 5 IS THE EASY PART

100% cotton T-shirt
Sizes L, XL
$15.00

ORDER FORM

Qty Title   Price/@   Total

____America's Daughters $16.95 _____

____"The Answer is NO" $13.95 _____

____Before Period $13.95 _____

____Good Friends $13.95 _____

____Planet Wampetter $15.00 _____

____Survival Tips $10.95 _____

____Win the Whining War $13.95 _____

____MomShirt size L or XL $15.00 _____

Subtotal _____

Tax (CA residents 8.25%)_____

Shipping ($4 for 1st , $1 for @ add'l)_____

TOTAL ENCLOSED _____

Name: _____

Organization: _____

Address: _____

City, State, Zip: _____

Phone: _____

Credit Card #: _____

Exp. Date: _____

Signature: _____

PERSPECTIVE PUBLISHING

Send to: Perspective Publishing, Inc.
2528 Sleepy Hollow Dr. #A • Glendale, CA 91206
Or call: 1-800-330-5851
Or order on the internet: www.familyhelp.com

More from Perspective Publishing

Perspective Publishing is a small independent publishing company which helps parents with the problems you face every day: discipline, friendship problems, talking with your kids, balancing work and family, challenging and inspiring your kids.

AMERICA'S DAUGHTERS: 400 Years of American Women
by Judith Head

This easy-to-read yet carefully researched history of American women from the 1600s to today is illustrated with 150 photos and period drawings, and gives children and adults both an overview of what life was like for women, and profiles of more than 50 individual women, both famous and not so well known.

    ISBN: 0-9622036-8-8 Paperback. 8"x10"; 128 pages; $16.95

Win the Whining War & Other Skirmishes: A family peace plan
by Cynthia Whitham, MSW

This easy-to-use guide helps parents increase cooperation and reduce conflict with children ages 2-12. Step-by-step, parents learn how to cut out all the annoying behavior (tantrums, teasing, dawdling, interrupting, complaining, etc.) that drives them crazy.

    ISBN: 0-9622036-3-7, paperback. 6"x9"; 208 pages; $13.95

"The Answer is NO": Saying it and sticking to it
by Cynthia Whitham, MSW

Tackling twenty-six situations that plague parents of 2 to 12-year-olds, this book helps parents define their values, build good parenting habits, and set firm, fair limits. Bedtime, pets, makeup, music, TV, homework, and designer clothes are just a few of the problems covered.

    ISBN: 0-9622036-4-5, paperback. 6"x9"; 224 pages; $13.95l

Survival Tips for Working Moms: 297 REAL Tips from REAL Moms
by Linda Goodman Pillsbury

Full of examples of how the tips actually work in real families, this is a light but no-nonsense practical resource thast can help every working mom. From chores to childcare, errands to exercise, this book makes life easier. Almost 100 cartoons make this a book you can't put down.

    ISBN: 0-9622036-5-3, paperback. 6"x9"; 192 pages; $10.95

Good Friends Are Hard to Find: Help your child find, make and keep friends
by Fred Frankel, Ph.D.

Step-by-step, parents learn to help their 5 to 12-year-olds make friends and solve problems with other kids. This guide also offers concrete help for teasing, bullying and meanness, both for the child who is picked on and for the tormentor. Based on UCLA's world renowned Children's Social Skills Program, this book teaches clinically tested techniques that really work.

    ISBN: 0-9622036-7-X, paperback. 6"x9"; 242 pages; $13.95

Order now: 1-800-330-5851 or www.familyhelp.com

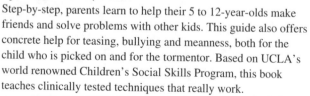

More from Perspective Publishing

Before She Gets Her Period: Talking to your daughter about menstruation
by Jessica B. Gillooly, Ph.D.
This friendly book has up-to-date information and uses real personal stories, exercises and activities to help parents talk with their daughters about menstruation — even if their daughters don't want to talk. It's the only book about menstruation written for parents.

   ISBN: 0-9622036-9-6, paperback. 6"x9"; 166 pages; $13.95

The Invasion of Planet Wampetter
by Samuel H. Pillsbury
Illustrated by Matthew Angorn

... Gertrude Tub save ... st trap in this ... taining for ... aloud.

   144 pages; $15.00

ART

ORDER
Qty Title

____Amer ... War $13.95 _____

____"The ... or XL $15.00 _____

____Befor ... Subtotal _____

____Goo ... idents 8.25%)_____

____Plan ... $1 for @ add'l)_____

____Surv ... L ENCLOSED _____

Organization: _____

Address: _____

City, State, Zip: _____

Phone: _____

Credit Card #: _____

Exp. Date: _____

Signature: _____

Send to: Perspective Publishing, Inc.
2528 Sleepy Hollow Dr. #A • Glendale, CA 91206
Or call: 1-800-330-5851
Or order on the internet: www.familyhelp.com

PERSPECTIVE PUBLISHING